BLA___ MADONNA

A Journey Through Her Faces, Myths, Mysteries Across Cultures and Sacred Practices of the Great Goddess

HENRIETTA MARTINEZ

Copyright and Disclaimer

Disclaimer:
This book is intended for informational and educational purposes only. The content reflects the author's personal experiences, research, and spiritual practices. It is not a substitute for professional advice, including legal, medical, psychological, or financial guidance. Readers are encouraged to use their own discretion and consult appropriate professionals as needed. The author is not liable for any outcomes resulting from the use of the information contained in this book.

The spiritual practices and rituals discussed in this book are meant to enhance personal growth and connection. Readers are advised to approach them with respect, mindfulness, and a commitment to safety, particularly when working with fire, herbs, or other tools. Always follow local laws and environmental guidelines when practicing outdoor rituals or leaving offerings.

By engaging with the content of this book, readers accept full responsibility for their actions and experiences. The author makes no guarantees about the efficacy of any practices or rituals described herein.

TESTIMONIALS

"This book is a masterpiece. It not only deepened my understanding of the Black Madonna but also transformed how I view the divine feminine. The blend of history, culture, and spirituality is unmatched—an absolute must-read for anyone seeking inspiration and empowerment."
— **Dr. Margaret Rosenthal**, Author and Spirituality Scholar

"I was captivated by the richness and depth of this book. The stories of the Black Madonna from different cultures resonated deeply with my own journey. This is not just a book; it's an invitation to connect with the sacred feminine in a way that feels both timeless and relevant."
— **Amara Toussaint**, Feminine Empowerment Coach

"Every page of this book is filled with wisdom and beauty. It honors the Black Madonna's complex and mysterious nature while making her relevance to modern life clear. I felt seen, inspired, and connected to something greater while reading this."
— **Sofia Hernandez**, Cultural Anthropologist

"This is the most comprehensive and heartfelt exploration of the Black Madonna I've ever encountered. It bridges the ancient and the modern in a way that feels seamless and illuminating. A perfect guide for spiritual seekers."
— **James LeClair**, Author of *The Sacred Shadow*

"Through stunning storytelling and careful research, this book made me feel like I was walking alongside the Black Madonna herself. The practical rituals and reflections included are invaluable for connecting with her energy. Highly recommended!"
— **Priya Narayan**, Healer and Retreat Facilitator

"A powerful celebration of the Black Madonna's enduring relevance across cultures. This book reminds us that the divine feminine is a force of resilience, creativity, and healing. It's beautifully written and deeply moving."
— **Elena Morales**, Artist and Devotee

"I couldn't put this book down. It helped me understand the importance of the Black Madonna not just as a religious symbol but as an archetype for our times. A profound and eye-opening read."
— **Michael Carter**, Spiritual Writer and Speaker

"This book is a gift to anyone yearning to reclaim the sacred feminine in their lives. The historical insights are fascinating, and the spiritual lessons are transformative. I found myself returning to passages again and again."
— **Rachel Song**, Founder of Sacred Feminine Circles

"An extraordinary book that bridges history, spirituality, and personal growth. The Black Madonna's mysteries come alive on

every page, *offering wisdom for both the curious and the devoted. A treasure for any spiritual library."*
— **Dr. Samuel Bennett**, Theologian

"This book is more than an exploration of the Black Madonna—it's a journey of self-discovery. It helped me connect with my own resilience and creativity. I feel empowered to honor both my shadow and light, thanks to this work."
— **Danielle Roberts**, Transformational Life Coach

HOW TO USE THE BOOK

Black Madonna: A Journey Through Her Faces, Myths, and Mysteries Across Cultures is more than just a book to read; it's an experience to have and repeat. It is intended to meet readers at various stages of their personal, spiritual, or intellectual development, providing insights and practices that can be applied in multiple ways. Whether you're a historian hoping to comprehend her cultural significance, a spiritual seeker yearning for connection, or someone fascinated by her enduring mystery, this book will help you understand and engage with the Black Madonna.

Exploring The Chapters

Each chapter is meticulously planned to highlight a specific aspect of the Black Madonna's story, symbolism, and significance. The chapters combine history, culture, spirituality, and practical application. You can read the book to see how her mysteries unfold throughout time, beginning with her historical roots and progressing to her relevance in the present world. Alternatively, you can skip to the chapters most relevant to your interests or questions.

For example, if you're interested in her position in feminine empowerment, start with the chapters that discuss her link to the sacred feminine and how she encourages strength and creativity. The life cycle and shadow work sections can provide helpful information and techniques if you are going through a personal change. The book is adaptable, allowing you to tailor it to your requirements.

Engaging With The Stories

The Black Madonna is a very personal and global symbol, and the stories told in the book depict her many faces from various civilizations. Take some time to think about the stories that have touched you personally. What teachings do they provide? How do they relate to your own life?

You should journal your thoughts as you read, noting any moments of clarity or questions that occur. The book promotes active engagement, making reading a journey of self-discovery and introspection. Use the questions and ideas offered in each chapter as prompts for personal reflection.

Using Practices And Rituals

The book includes practical exercises, rituals, and meditations inspired by the Black Madonna. These techniques will help you connect with her energy and apply daily lessons.

1. Rituals for healing and transformation. Use these techniques to release old habits, heal emotional scars, or embrace rejuvenation. They offer a practical opportunity to connect with her energy and implement her teachings in your life.

2. darkness Work Exercises: The Black Madonna's link to the darkness might help you explore your hidden areas. Use these activities to address your concerns, embrace vulnerability, and turn problems into opportunities.

3. Altars and Sacred Places: If you are encouraged to strengthen your relationship, follow the instructions for

making a Black Madonna altar. This can be a focal point for prayer, meditation, and thought.

4. Prayers and Meditations: The book offers prayers and meditations for daily use or times of need. Use them to call upon her presence, seek advice, or find comfort in her loving energy.

These methods are designed to be accessible and adaptive. Choose the ones that speak to you, and feel free to edit them to reflect your unique views or spiritual path.

For Individual and Group Study

The book can serve as both a personal guide and a resource for collective exploration. It provides individuals a private room to contemplate, heal, and grow. It is an excellent resource for group discussions, rituals, and collaborative discovery of the Black Madonna's knowledge.

Consider using the book to organize group activities if you belong to a book club, a women's circle, or a spiritual organization. Discussing the Black Madonna's stories and themes can stimulate significant discussions and broaden our understanding. Group rituals or meditations inspired by the book can foster a sense of community and purpose.

Revisiting The Book

The Black Madonna's mysteries are broad and multilayered, and this book is meant to develop with you. What calls to you now may take on new meaning as your journey progresses. Revisit the chapters, stories, and practices throughout time to gain a better understanding and connection.

For example, if you read the book during personal development, the chapters on birth, death, and rebirth may hit home. Returning to the book, you may be drawn to the sections about her cultural significance or activity. The book's adaptability enables it to remain a relevant and inspiring resource at many stages of life.

Integrating Her Wisdom.

This book's ultimate objective is to inspire transformation rather than inform. The Black Madonna's teachings emphasize resilience, creativity, and balance, and the book offers practical strategies for living these virtues. As you work through the content, evaluate how her lessons can influence your actions, relationships, and worldview.

1. Personal Growth: Consider how her teachings can support your inner journey. Are there any elements of your life that require mending or renewal? How can you face the cycle of change with courage and grace?

2. Community Connection: The Black Madonna represents inclusivity and justice. How might her example motivate you to give back to your community, lift others, and create spaces for healing and connection?

3. Spiritual Practice: Her energy can strengthen your connection to the divine, whether you have a long-standing practice or are starting. Use the book's prayers, meditations, and rituals to support your spiritual journey.

A Guide For Life's Transitions

This book is handy during transition, uncertainty, or growth periods. The Black Madonna archetype provides direction for handling life's obstacles, from personal struggles to collective calamities. Use the book when you need clarity, comfort, or refreshment, and trust that her wisdom will illuminate the path ahead.

In times of struggle, go to the sections on her link to shadow and healing. Consider her role in creativity and feminine strength when looking for inspiration or empowerment. Consider her role in social justice and cultural progress when looking for purpose in the bigger picture.

Final Thoughts

Black Madonna: A Tour of Her Faces, Myths, and Mysteries Across Cultures is more than just a book; it's a resource for connecting, reflecting, and growing. It invites you to connect with the Black Madonna's knowledge in a personalized and meaningful way, tailoring her teachings to your specific life and circumstances. By actively engaging with this book— through reading, thought, and practice—you create a space for transformation and deepen your connection to this ageless icon of the divine feminine.

Whether you approach the book as a researcher, seeker, or devotee, it has something valuable for everyone. Let it serve as a guide, a source of inspiration, and a reminder that the sacred is constantly present, ready to be discovered. May the Black Madonna's lessons help you find strength in the dark, light in the journey, and wisdom in each stride ahead.

TABLE OF CONTENTS

INTRODUCTION

"Across centuries, her presence has remained unwavering—through wars, whispers, and winds of change, the Black Madonna stands as a beacon of enduring power."

The Black Madonna, a figure of global and timeless significance, has captivated people for decades. She is found in shrines, artwork, and legends, often standing out from the more familiar images of the Virgin Mary. Unlike the light-skinned and serene Mary of traditional Christian depictions, the Black Madonna is portrayed with a deep, earthy presence that exudes strength, mystery, and power. Her dark skin has sparked interest, devotion, and debate, inspiring individuals from diverse backgrounds. Across nations and generations, the Black Madonna has symbolized faith, resilience, and the sacred bond between humanity and the divine.

The Black Madonna is more than just a religious icon; she symbolizes an ancient and global relationship to the feminine divine. Her image can be found in France, Spain, Haiti, and Brazil under several names, including Notre Dame de Sous-Terre, Nuestra Señora de Montserrat, Our Lady of Aparecida, and Erzulie Dantor. Each rendition represents the traditions, challenges, and hopes of those who revere her. Despite her various incarnations, the Black Madonna conveys a message of power, maternal care, and transformation that transcends time and culture.

The origins of the Black Madonna are shrouded in mystery and folklore. Some regard her as a portrayal of the Virgin Mary, modified to meet diverse communities' cultural and spiritual needs. Others believe she resembles earlier goddesses who were adored long before Christianity. Her dark skin is frequently understood in several ways: as a symbol of her connection to the soil, a reflection of humility, or a reminder that the holy may be found in all places, including those we often overlook. Her image challenges traditional notions of holiness, inviting us to perceive divinity in light and shadows, where development and rebirth frequently begin.

Throughout history, the Black Madonna has been a beacon of hope for those facing adversity. She has served as a protector of the underprivileged, a guide for the oppressed, and a healer for the wounded. In Haiti, she emerged as a symbol of liberation for enslaved people, blending with African spiritual traditions to represent power and freedom. In Brazil, she is viewed as a mother who unites people of different races and classes. She stands as a powerful symbol of feminine strength, inspiring women to believe in their resilience and their ability to create and nurture.

Her effect extends beyond religion. The Black Madonna has inspired several art, literature, and music works. Writers and painters have considered her a symbol of metamorphosis and mystery. Her presence in their work illustrates her lasting relevance, demonstrating how she continues to impart wisdom in novel and creative ways. In contemporary concerns of identity, race, and gender, she serves as a reminder of the value of diversity and the power of inclusion. Her image challenges limiting ideas of beauty and holiness, urging us to embrace a more expansive understanding of what it is to be human and divine.

To truly understand the Black Madonna, we must explore her from multiple perspectives. She embodies layers of meaning shaped by the history, culture, and spirituality of those who worship her. In France, she is linked to revered pilgrimage routes and the mysteries of ancient churches. In Spain, she is known as La Moreneta, a beloved guardian whose shrine is nestled in the highlands of Montserrat. She is a potent defender of Vodou's beliefs in Haiti, symbolizing justice and strength. In Brazil, she is the unifying figure for Nossa Senhora Aparecida, the country's patron saint. Each of these manifestations illustrates how the Black Madonna responds to the needs and struggles of those who revere her, transcending cultural and geographical boundaries.

Despite her pervasive presence, the Black Madonna remains unexplained. Scholars have contested her origins, with some claiming she represents early portrayals of Mary that emphasized her connection to regular people and the soil. Others think she reflects the survival of pre-Christian goddess traditions that have gradually been incorporated into Christian images. Some consider her black appearance a purposeful deviation from European notions of divinity, making her a symbol of inclusiveness and representation. Regardless of these interpretations, the Black Madonna invites us to reconsider our concepts of the sacred and to experience divinity in new and inclusive ways.

Today, the Black Madonna remains a powerful and relevant icon. She offers guidance and hope in a society grappling with environmental crises, social injustices, and spiritual disconnection. Her dark hue symbolizes the earth's cycles of birth and death, while her association with the oppressed underscores the importance of solidarity and justice. As a figure of metamorphosis, she inspires us to confront our fears and hardships, believing that regeneration is possible even in the darkest times. She encourages us to reclaim the divine feminine by fostering balance and creativity in our lives and communities, making her a figure of engagement and connection to current issues.

This book is about experiencing the Black Madonna rather than simply researching her. She is not confined to history books or religious writings but exists in the hearts of people seeking her. Each chapter delves into a different facet of Mary, from her historical background to her spiritual significance. We'll look at how she influenced art, culture, activism, and the practices and rituals that help individuals connect with her spirit. These experiences and thoughts will demonstrate how the Black Madonna continues to inspire devotion and transformation.

The Black Madonna is more than just a figure to admire; she is a presence that inspires us to contemplate, learn, and take action. She encourages us to embrace all aspects of ourselves—light and shadow, joy and pain—and to find strength in our problems. Her message is ageless and universal: the sacred exists in all aspects of life, and transformation is always possible. As we explore her various faces, stories, and mysteries, we may discover that the Black Madonna is more than simply a remote figure; she is a guide who speaks directly to our hearts and lives.

1: THE UNIVERSAL ARCHETYPE OF THE BLACK MADONNA

"In the face of adversity, the Black Madonna whispers courage to those who listen, showing that from the darkest moments, light can emerge."

THE ROOTS OF THE DIVINE DARK MOTHER

For centuries, the Black Madonna has stood as a mysterious and powerful figure, her dark skin a symbol of shadow and light, her presence deeply rooted in the archetype of the Divine Dark Mother. She is not simply a religious figure; she is an archetype that transcends cultures, faiths, and traditions. To understand her fully, one must journey back to the ancient goddesses who first embodied the sacred feminine in its multi-faceted forms—goddesses like Isis, Kali, and Inanna, who laid the foundation for the Black Madonna's enduring power.

Origins Of The Dark Mother Archetype

The archetype of the Dark Mother is ancient, predating recorded history, yet her energy is timeless and universal. She represents the paradox of life: She is both nurturing and fierce, comforting and challenging, creator and destroyer.

These qualities are often misunderstood in the modern world, but they speak to the depth of human experience—the highs and lows, the joys and sorrows, the duality of existence itself.

The Wisdom Of Isis: The Mother Of Rebirth

In ancient Egypt, the goddess Isis was revered as the mother of all creation. She was the bringer of life and the protector of the dead, her power rooted in her ability to navigate the liminal spaces between life and death. Her story, which tells of her piecing together the dismembered body of her husband Osiris and resurrecting him, is not just mythology—it is a profound spiritual metaphor.

In real life, many of us feel as though we are piecing together parts of ourselves after loss, heartbreak, or trauma. Isis reminds us that there is power in persistence, in gathering the scattered pieces of our lives and creating something whole again. She embodies the energy of rebirth and renewal, and her influence is evident in the Black Madonna, who, like Isis, holds the paradox of life and death within her dark embrace.

Practical Takeaway:

When life feels fractured, take time to gather your pieces intentionally. Write down what you think you've lost—whether it's a sense of purpose, joy, or connection. Then, list one small action you can take daily to reclaim these pieces. Think of Isis as you do this: each small step is an act of divine creation.

Kali: The Fierce Protector And Destroyer Of Illusion

In Hindu mythology, Kali is the dark-skinned goddess of transformation and destruction. She is terrifying to behold, with her wild hair, fierce eyes, and a necklace of skulls. Yet Kali's destruction is not chaos—it is purpose-driven. She destroys illusions, ego, and anything that no longer serves the soul's growth.

The Black Madonna echoes Kali's ferocity. She challenges us to face the truth, even when it is uncomfortable or painful. Like Kali, the Black Madonna protects the oppressed, the grieving, and the vulnerable. Her darkness is not to be feared but embraced, for it reveals what must change to allow transformation.

Practical Takeaway:

Think of a part of your life that feels stagnant or out of alignment. What illusions are you clinging to? Write these down and consider how releasing them might free you to grow. You can create a small ritual, like lighting a candle, to symbolize letting go of what no longer serves you, calling on Kali's fierce energy to guide you.

Inanna: The Queen Of Heaven And The Descent Into Darkness

Inanna, the Sumerian goddess of love, fertility, and war, is perhaps the most profound representation of the Dark Mother archetype. Her myth of descent into the underworld speaks to embracing the shadow self. Inanna willingly descends into darkness, stripping herself of her royal garments and symbols of power at each gate until she stands naked before the underworld queen. Her story is one of surrender, transformation, and eventual ascension.

The Black Madonna carries this same energy of descent and resurrection. She invites us to confront our fears and vulnerabilities, shed our ego layers, and stand authentically in our truth. Like Inanna, she teaches us that only by facing our shadow can we emerge renewed and empowered.

Practical Takeaway:

Consider when you faced a personal "descent"—a period of struggle or loss. Reflect on what this experience taught you and how it transformed you. Write about this in a journal, embracing the lessons of Inanna and the Black Madonna. If you are currently in a challenging time, remember that descent is often the first step to rebirth.

Embracing The Dark Mother Today

The Dark Mother archetype, embodied by figures like Isis, Kali, and Inanna, reminds us of the sacredness of all parts of life—the dark and the light. The Black Madonna carries this legacy, urging us to embrace our strength and vulnerability, our joy and our pain.

When you honor the Black Madonna, you celebrate the parts of yourself that have been overlooked, suppressed, or judged. You are reclaiming your power, just as these ancient goddesses remind us to do. Whether through prayer, meditation, or simple self-reflection, connecting with this archetype can be a profoundly healing and transformative experience.

Each step you take toward honoring the Divine Dark Mother

is a step toward becoming whole. And in her wisdom, you will find healing and the courage to walk through life with grace, resilience, and strength.

THEMES OF DARKNESS, TRANSFORMATION, AND CREATION

With her enigmatic presence and profound symbolism, the Black Madonna embodies the intricate dance of life's cycles: death, transformation, and rebirth. Her dark visage invites us to step into the shadows, not as a place of fear but as a sacred space where the alchemy of the soul unfolds. To truly understand her, we must embrace her wisdom in these themes—darkness as a source of creation, transformation as a necessary passage, and rebirth as the ultimate renewal.

How The Black Madonna Symbolizes Cycles Of Death And Rebirth

The Black Madonna's symbolism of darkness often stirs discomfort. Darkness is too often equated with endings, loss, or fear of the unknown. But within her shadowy embrace lies the same fertile darkness of the soil, where seeds are planted, and life begins anew. She is not just a figure of endings but the keeper of beginnings.

Darkness As Fertile Ground For Growth

The Black Madonna reminds us that darkness is where creation begins. Just as a seed must be buried in the soil to sprout, so must we often retreat into our inner darkness to grow. This is not a journey of escape but introspection and discovery.

Take the moon's cycles as an example. In its dark phase, the moon is invisible to the eye, yet it is in this stillness that the cycle begins anew. The Black Madonna mirrors this lunar rhythm, teaching us that what appears to be an ending is, in truth, the start of something new.

Practical Advice:

When faced with uncertainty or change, instead of resisting, take a moment to pause and reflect. Ask yourself: *What new beginning might be hiding in this ending?* Spend time journaling or meditating in darkness—perhaps lighting a single candle as a reminder that light emerges from the dark.

Transformation Through Trials

The Black Madonna embodies the process of transformation through challenges. Life's most transformative moments are rarely easy—they often demand we shed old versions of ourselves. This is the essence of her presence: She walks with us through life's trials, holding space for the pain of letting go and the beauty of what lies beyond.

Consider the caterpillar's metamorphosis into a butterfly. The caterpillar must completely dissolve within the cocoon before transforming into something entirely new. The Black Madonna mirrors this process, urging us to surrender to the transformation that comes with life's difficulties.

Practical Advice:

When facing a trial, try to reframe it as a cocoon—a temporary space for transformation. Write down what part of yourself is dissolving and what you hope will emerge. This acknowledgment can help you trust the process and stay grounded in faith.

Rebirth As A Sacred Renewal

Rebirth is perhaps the most beautiful theme embodied by the Black Madonna. Just as the phoenix rises from its ashes, the Black Madonna shows us that there is an ascension into light after every descent into darkness. Her symbolism encourages us to embrace the cycles of life, trusting that every ending carries the seeds of renewal within it.

In practical terms, this can mean starting over after loss—a new career, a relationship, or even a sense of self. Rebirth isn't about forgetting the past but integrating its lessons into a more vibrant, authentic version of yourself.

Real-World Example:

Think of a time when you emerged more vigorous after a challenging experience. It may be the Bethe job loss that led to a new, fulfilling career or a painful breakup that helped you discover your true worth. These moments of rebirth are your connection to the Black Madonna, who guides us through such cycles.

Practical Advice:

Create a ritual to honor your cycles of rebirth. Light a candle and reflect on where you've been and how far you've come.

Speak aloud what you are stepping into, affirming your readiness to embrace this next chapter of your life.

A Sacred Invitation

The Black Madonna calls us to see the beauty in life's cycles, even when difficult. She reminds us that darkness is not an ending but a beginning, transformation is not destruction but growth, and rebirth is the promise that life continues, more vibrant and accurate than before.

In her presence, we are invited to trust the rhythms of life, knowing that within every challenge lies the potential for profound renewal. Through her wisdom, we are reminded that even in our darkest moments, we are never truly alone—there is always light waiting to be reborn.

WHY DARKNESS IS SACRED

Why Darkness Is Sacred

In a world that often glorifies light as the ultimate goal—happiness, clarity, and certainty—darkness is seen as something to avoid, suppress, or fear. Yet the Black Madonna challenges this perspective. She reminds us that darkness is not the absence of power or wisdom but its origin. To truly embrace spirituality, we must reclaim the sacredness of shadow energy, for it is within the darkness that profound transformation, creativity, and healing take root, offering us a beacon of hope and inspiration.

Reclaiming The Power And Wisdom Of Shadow Energy In Spirituality

Darkness as a Source of Creation

Think of the womb. It is one of the most sacred spaces—dark, hidden, and nurturing. Within its quiet depths, life is formed and sustained. This is the essence of holy darkness: potential resides where the seeds of new ideas, paths, and ways of being begin to take shape.

The Black Madonna embodies this creative power. Her darkness is not barren or empty—it is full of possibilities waiting to be brought into the light. When we turn inward to embrace our inner darkness, we connect with this same source of creation.

Practical Advice:

The next time you feel stuck or uninspired, try a practice of "intentional stillness." This is a deliberate act of creating a quiet, dark space for introspection and self-discovery. Turn off all distractions, dim the lights, and sit in silence for a few minutes. Imagine that within this darkness lies the potential for your next breakthrough—creatively, spiritually, or emotionally. Use this time to explore your thoughts and feelings, to listen to your inner voice, and to connect with your shadow self. This practice can be a powerful tool for personal growth and self-discovery.

Embracing the Shadow Self

The Black Madonna invites us to face the parts of ourselves

that we hide, deny, or push away—the shadow self. This includes unresolved emotions, fears, and parts of our identity that are unacceptable or unlovable. But it is only by embracing these shadows that we can become whole.

Consider this: the shadow is not inherently evil; it is simply the part of you that hasn't been fully integrated. Ignoring it only allows it to grow in power, often manifesting as self-sabotage, resentment, or fear. The Black Madonna's wisdom lies in showing us that by facing our shadows with compassion, we can reclaim their power and wisdom.

Real-World Example:

Imagine someone who struggles with anger. Instead of repressing it, they explore it—journaling, meditating, or speaking with a therapist. In doing so, they discover that beneath their anger is a deep desire for boundaries and respect. By honoring this need, they transform anger from a destructive force into a guide for self-respect and empowerment.

Practical Advice:

Identify one part of your shadow self—a fear, habit, or

emotion you've been avoiding. Spend time journaling about its root cause and what it might be trying to teach you. Approach this exercise with curiosity, not judgment. Then, take a step towards integrating this part of yourself into your daily life. This could be as simple as acknowledging the fear when it arises, or consciously choosing a different response to the triggering situation.

Darkness As A Path To Spiritual Growth

In spiritual traditions worldwide, darkness is often seen as the entry point to enlightenment. The mystics of Christianity, the seekers of Eastern traditions, and the shamans of indigenous cultures all recognize the importance of the "night of the soul"—a period of spiritual emptiness or struggle that leads to profound growth and connection with the divine. This 'night of the soul' is a transformative experience, a period of intense self-examination and reflection, often marked by feelings of despair and hopelessness. It is a necessary step on the path to spiritual growth, as it forces us to confront our deepest fears and insecurities, and ultimately leads to a deeper connection with the divine.

The Black Madonna represents this journey. She reminds us that spiritual growth is not linear, and we often discover our greatest strength and wisdom in our most difficult moments. Her presence serves as a comforting guide, supporting us through the darkness and into a deeper connection with ourselves and the divine.

Real-World Example:

Think of times when life felt overwhelming—perhaps the loss of a loved one, the end of a relationship, or a period of uncertainty. These moments, while painful, often force us to grow in ways we never imagined. Like the Black Madonna, they guide us through the darkness and into a deeper connection with ourselves and the divine.

Practical Advice:

When facing a difficult period, reframe it as a "night of the soul." Write down what this experience might teach you about yourself, your needs, and your path. Trust that, like the Black Madonna. You will emerge more substantially and aligned from this darkness.

The Sacred Invitation Of Darkness

The Black Madonna teaches us that darkness is not a punishment or a failure—it is sacred. It is where life begins, transformation occurs, and the most profound truths about ourselves are revealed. To embrace the wisdom of the Black Madonna is to embrace your darkness, trusting that within it lies the power to create, heal, and grow.

When you reclaim the sacredness of darkness, you step into a deeper, more authentic spirituality—one that honors all parts of yourself, not just the light. In doing so, you find a sense of wholeness, power, and peace that can only come from walking through the shadows with courage and grace. Embracing darkness is not a sign of weakness, but a testament to your strength and resilience.

2: FACES OF THE BLACK MADONNA IN EUROPE

"The Black Madonna teaches us that our true strength lies in embracing all parts of ourselves—light and dark, soft and fierce, human and divine."

REVERED ICONS OF THE SACRED FEMININE

THE BLACK MADONNA OF CZESTOCHOWA

Nestled in the Jasna Góra Monastery in Czestochowa, Poland stands one of the most iconic and revered depictions of the Black Madonna. Known as *Our Lady of Czestochowa,* this sacred image has drawn millions of pilgrims over the centuries, offering them solace, strength, and a deep connection to the divine. Both a religious icon and a cultural symbol, she holds a unique place in Polish history, spirituality, and identity.

Historical Significance In Poland

The origins of the Black Madonna of Czestochowa are steeped in both legend and history. According to tradition, the painting was created by Saint Luke the Evangelist on a cedar wood panel, believed to have come from a table used by the Holy Family. Eventually, the icon was brought to Poland in the 14th century by Prince Władysław Opolczyk, who entrusted it to the care of the Jasna Góra Monastery.

Poland, a nation that has faced centuries of turmoil, invasion, and struggle, has consistently turned to the Black Madonna as a symbol of protection and hope. During the Swedish Deluge in the 17th century, the monastery became a fortress of resistance, and the Black Madonna was credited with helping a small group of Polish defenders hold off a massive Swedish army. Since then, she has been affectionately known as the "Queen of Poland," and her image is seen as a guardian of the nation, a constant source of security and reassurance.

Her scars—two distinctive slashes on her right cheek—tell their story of resilience. Legend has it that during an invasion, a group of robbers attempted to desecrate the icon, and despite their efforts to repair it, the scars mysteriously reappeared. These marks symbolize the suffering of the Polish people and their unwavering faith through adversity.

Spiritual Significance

The Black Madonna of Czestochowa is not merely an icon; she is seen as an intercessor, a healer, and a guide for the faithful. Her dark visage conveys mystery, strength, and universality, making her a source of comfort for people from all walks of life. Pilgrims often report feelings of profound peace and spiritual renewal in her presence.

In the Catholic tradition, she represents Mary as the protector of humanity. Yet her darkness and the scars on her face give her an added depth—she resonates with those who have suffered, struggled, and endured. Her appearance seems to say, "I understand your pain, and I will walk you through it."

Practical Example:

Take the story of a modern pilgrim, Agnieszka, who journeyed to Jasna Góra to seek clarity during a difficult divorce. Standing before the Black Madonna, she prayed for strength and guidance. She later described feeling an unexplainable calm and a renewed sense of purpose. For her, the Black Madonna wasn't just an image; she became a personal source of resilience.

Lessons for Feminine Empowerment

The Black Madonna of Czestochowa holds special significance for feminine empowerment. Her strength as a protector, her scars as a testament to survival, and her ability to inspire devotion all speak to women's power to endure and thrive through life's challenges. She embodies resilience, nurturing energy, and fierce protection—a potent combination of traits that make her a role model for modern women seeking to reclaim their power, inspiring and motivating them to face life's challenges with courage.

Practical Advice:

If you feel disconnected from your inner strength, meditate on the image of the Black Madonna of Czestochowa. Visualize her scars as reminders that beauty and power often come from the trials we endure. Journal about a time when you faced adversity and how it shaped you. Honor those moments as sacred markers of your resilience.

A Timeless Symbol Of Hope

The Black Madonna of Czestochowa is more than a religious figure; she symbolizes hope, strength, and unity. For centuries, she has stood as a beacon for those in need, offering spiritual guidance and a deep connection to the sacred feminine. Whether you see her as a protector, a healer, or a reminder of your resilience, her presence invites you to embrace the strength and wisdom in life's challenges.

As she continues to inspire millions, the Black Madonna of Czestochowa reminds us that even in the darkest moments, there is light to be found—and that scars, both visible and invisible, are often the greatest testaments to the beauty of the human spirit.

OUR LADY OF MONTSERRAT (LA MORENETA)

High atop the rocky peaks of Montserrat in Catalonia, Spain, sits a shrine dedicated to *La Moreneta,* or the "Little Dark One." Known as Our Lady of Montserrat, she is one of Europe's most revered Black Madonnas, drawing pilgrims worldwide to seek her blessings. Her significance lies not only in her spiritual role but also in her deep connection to Catalan identity and the rich history of Spain.

Her Role As A Protector In Spain's Spiritual History

The origins of Our Lady of Montserrat are steeped in mystery. According to legend, shepherd boys discovered her statue in a cave on Montserrat's jagged mountainside in the 9th century.

Guided by a miraculous light, they found the small, dark-skinned statue hidden deep within the cave. When locals attempted to move her to a nearby village, the statue became impossibly heavy—a clear sign that she wished to remain on the mountain.

Montserrat soon became a pilgrimage site, and a monastery was built to honor her. Over the centuries, Our Lady of Montserrat came to be viewed as a powerful protector. Her presence was said to bring healing, strength, and miracles to those who sought her aid.

During the Spanish Civil War, Montserrat became a symbol of resilience. The monastery, threatened by destruction, stood firm, and La Moreneta's image offered hope to the people amidst political and social turmoil. Even today, she is seen as a guardian of Catalonia, embodying the strength and endurance of its people.

Practical Example:

During one particularly turbulent period in the 20th century, locals would quietly make their way to Montserrat despite the dangers, lighting candles and praying before La Moreneta. Her role as a protector wasn't just symbolic—it gave people hope and courage in times of fear and uncertainty.

Spiritual Significance Of La Moreneta

At first glance, the statue of La Moreneta might seem small, even unassuming. She is a seated figure, her dark complexion contrasting with the golden accents of her throne. Yet her presence is anything but ordinary. The statue radiates an energy of quiet power, her compassionate and commanding gaze.

La Moreneta is often associated with healing, particularly of the heart and spirit. Pilgrims frequently climb the winding paths of Montserrat to stand before her, leaving behind offerings, lighting candles, and praying for guidance. Her connection to the natural world—symbolized by her placement high in the mountains—underscores her role as a mediator between humanity and the divine.

Real-World Example:

A pilgrim named María, recovering from a serious illness, made the arduous trek to Montserrat. Standing before La Moreneta, she described feeling an overwhelming sense of calm and strength, as if the statue assured her that she was not alone in her struggle. In the following months, María credited her recovery to medicine and the renewed faith she found at Montserrat.

Practical Advice:

If you feel overwhelmed by life's challenges, consider connecting with the energy of La Moreneta. You don't have to be in Montserrat to feel her presence—light a candle in a quiet space, reflect on her image, and ask for her guidance. Imagine her strength becoming your own, a protective force that helps you navigate difficulties.

A Symbol Of Feminine Strength And Protection

La Moreneta embodies the qualities of feminine strength and

protection. She is a nurturing figure, yet she is also unyielding—a force to be reckoned with when defending those in need. Her role in Spain's history reflects this duality. As Catalonia's spiritual protector, she has served as a unifying figure, helping to preserve cultural identity in the face of adversity.

Practical Example:

Her influence extends beyond spiritual realms into daily life. Catalan women, for example, often view her as a source of inspiration when facing personal or societal challenges. Her enduring presence reminds us that true strength lies in the balance of compassion and resilience.

Practical Advice:

Think of a situation where you've had to balance nurturing and strength. Write about this experience in a journal, reflecting on what it taught you. Visualize La Moreneta's steady presence as a source of guidance and protection as you move forward.

A Mountain Of Faith And Mystery

Our Lady of Montserrat, La Moreneta, is more than a religious statue; she is a timeless protector, healer, and symbol of strength. Like other Black Madonnas, her dark skin carries a profound message: the sacred is not always found in the light but often in the mysterious depths of life.

For centuries, she has watched over the mountains of Montserrat, a beacon of faith and resilience for those who climb to meet her. Whether you connect with her as a spiritual guide, a cultural symbol, or a source of inspiration, La Moreneta offers an invitation to find strength in your struggles, trust the journey, and embrace the mysteries of life with an open heart.

THE NOTRE DAME OF CHARTRES CATHEDRAL

Amid the sweeping Gothic arches and stunning stained-glass windows of the Notre Dame Cathedral in Chartres, France lies one of the most enigmatic and revered depictions of the Black Madonna. Known as *Our Lady of the Underground,* she resides in a crypt beneath the grand cathedral, a place of quiet mystery and profound spiritual significance. For centuries, this sacred figure has drawn pilgrims seeking solace, healing, and the wisdom of the divine feminine. Her presence at Chartres is steeped in symbolism and shrouded in fascinating mysteries.

The Symbolism Of The Black Madonna At Chartres

The Black Madonna of Chartres represents nurturing, fertility, and the sacred feminine. She is often depicted holding the Christ child, her dark visage a striking contrast to the cathedral's luminous surroundings. This contrast is no accident—it serves to highlight her role as a bridge between light and shadow, between humanity and the divine.

Her placement in the crypt symbolizes her connection to the earth, emphasizing her association with the ancient goddess archetypes tied to fertility and the cycles of nature. Many believe the cathedral site was once a pagan sanctuary dedicated to a mother goddess. In this way, the Black Madonna continues the sacred feminine's presence, blending ancient traditions with Christian devotion.

The symbolism extends to the cathedral itself. Chartres is renowned for its labyrinth, a winding path that mirrors the spiritual journey. Pilgrims often meditate on this labyrinth, connecting with the wisdom of the Black Madonna as they navigate its twists and turns. She becomes a guide through life's uncertainties, helping seekers find clarity and inner peace.

Practical Advice:

If you are feeling lost or unsure of your path, consider meditating on the image of a labyrinth. Envision the Black Madonna as your guide, helping you navigate the complexities of your journey. Trust that there is purpose and meaning even in the twists and turns.

The Mysteries Of The Black Madonna At Chartres

The Black Madonna at Chartres is surrounded by legends and

mysteries that deepen her allure. One of the most fascinating aspects is the belief that the crypt lies on an ancient sacred site where Druids once worshipped a fertility goddess known as "Virgo Paritura" (the Virgin Who Will Give Birth). This connection suggests that the Black Madonna may have absorbed some of this ancient tradition's spiritual energy and significance, serving as a bridge between pagan and Christian devotion.

Another mystery lies in her dark skin. Some suggest it symbolizes the fertility of the earth, while others interpret it as a reflection of the divine's universal and inclusive nature. Her darkness reminds us that sacredness transcends physical appearances, cultural boundaries, and conventional notions of purity.

Even the cathedral's alignment with celestial patterns adds to the intrigue. It is said that the structure is built on ley lines, or energy pathways, that amplify spiritual experiences. Pilgrims often report feeling an unexplainable sense of peace, healing, or transformation in the crypt, as though the Black Madonna is channeling this energy.

Real-World Example:

A French teacher named Jeanne visited Chartres during a profound personal crisis. While sitting in the crypt before the Black Madonna, she felt an overwhelming sense of calm and clarity. Jeanne later described the experience as a "rebirth," crediting the Black Madonna with helping her reconnect with her purpose and confidence.

Practical Advice:

If you cannot visit Chartres, you can still connect with the energy of the Black Madonna. Create a quiet space in your home where you can sit in reflection. Use an image or a candle to represent her presence and meditate on the mysteries she embodies.

Her Role As A Feminine Protector And Guide

As a representation of the sacred feminine, the Black Madonna at Chartres is seen as a protector, particularly for those seeking to reclaim their inner strength or find their way through challenging times. Her placement in the crypt—a place of quiet retreat—emphasizes her role as a guide in the introspective, transformative journey.

Unlike divine feminine figures emphasizing purity or gentleness, the Black Madonna embodies resilience and balance. She holds space for both joy and sorrow, for light and shadow, reminding us that life's challenges are integral to the spiritual path.

Practical Advice:

Reflect on a time when you overcame a significant challenge. How did that experience shape you? Write down what you learned and how you grew. Think of the Black Madonna as a witness to your strength and transformation, a guide encouraging you to continue embracing life's complexities.

A Sacred Presence In The Heart Of France

The Black Madonna of Chartres is more than a statue; she is a

symbol of spiritual depth, mystery, and transformation. Her placement in the crypt ties her to the earth's grounding energy, while her history connects her to the ancient wisdom of the sacred feminine.

Through her symbolism and mysteries, she invites us to embrace the fullness of our humanity—the light and the dark, the known and the unknown. Whether as a protector, a guide, or a reminder of life's sacred cycles, she continues to inspire and transform all who seek her wisdom.

3: THE BLACK MADONNA IN AFRICA AND THE MIDDLE EAST

"The Black Madonna is not just a figure of worship but a living embodiment of all that is sacred, powerful, and mysterious in the world."

THE DARK MOTHER'S ANCIENT ROOTS

ISIS AS THE ORIGINAL BLACK MADONNA

The ancient Egyptian goddess Isis holds a foundational role in the lineage of the Black Madonna. Often depicted as a mother holding her child, Horus, Isis embodies qualities of protection, creation, and divine wisdom that directly influenced the development of later spiritual traditions. Her image, her stories, and her widespread reverence across cultures laid the groundwork for the archetype of the Dark Mother that the Black Madonna represents today.

Connection To Ancient Egyptian Mythology

In Egyptian mythology, Isis is a goddess of immense power and a devoted mother. Her story is one of love, resilience, and mystical ability. When her husband Osiris was murdered and dismembered by his brother Set, Isis searched tirelessly to find the scattered pieces of his body. Using her magical knowledge, she resurrected Osiris long enough to conceive their child, Horus, who would go on to avenge his father and restore balance to the cosmos.

This story of death, resurrection, and motherhood mirrors many of the themes we associate with the Black Madonna. Like Isis, the Black Madonna embodies the strength to navigate life's darkness and emerge with renewed purpose. Both figures represent the divine feminine as a force of creation and transformation.

The image of Isis nursing her infant son, Horus, became a powerful symbol in Egyptian art. Over time, this depiction influenced early Christian representations of Mary holding the Christ child. Many scholars believe that as Christianity spread through Egypt and the Mediterranean, Isis's attributes and iconography were absorbed into the figure of Mary, contributing to the later development of the Black Madonna's imagery.

Isis's Influence On Later Traditions

Isis was not confined to Egypt; her worship spread far beyond its borders, influencing spiritual traditions in Greece, Rome, and even as far as the British Isles. Temples dedicated to Isis dotted the ancient world, and her followers revered her as a universal mother figure who transcended cultural boundaries.

In later traditions, her influence became interwoven with Christian beliefs. Early depictions of the Virgin Mary in North

Africa and the Middle East often show her with dark skin, a visual and symbolic link to Isis. These Black Madonnas, like Isis, represent the nurturing and protective qualities of the divine feminine and the sacred mysteries of life, death, and rebirth.

Isis's influence can also be seen in her connection to the natural world. She was associated with the Nile, the cycles of fertility, and the stars—especially the star Sirius, which marked the flooding of the Nile and the renewal of life. Similarly, the Black Madonna is often tied to natural elements, emphasizing her role as a protector of the earth and its cycles.

Practical Lessons From Isis's Legacy

The story of Isis offers powerful lessons for modern life. Her resilience in the face of loss, unwavering devotion, and ability to transform despair into renewal can inspire us to navigate our challenges with grace and determination. These practical lessons from her legacy can empower us to face our own struggles with renewed strength and inspiration.

Practical Advice:

- **Resilience in Difficult Times:** When faced with hardship, reflect on Isis's journey to find and resurrect Osiris. Write down one action today to reclaim a sense of balance or hope.

- **Mothering Energy:** Whether you are a parent or nurturing a creative project, channel Isis's energy by meditating on her image. Imagine yourself as both protector and creator, fostering growth and transformation.

- **Connection to Nature:** Spend time outdoors to honor the natural cycles Isis represents. Whether by walking barefoot on the earth, gazing at the stars, or meditating by water, reconnect with the sacred rhythms of life.

The Timeless Presence Of Isis

Isis's legacy as the original Black Madonna endures, a testament to the timeless influence of her archetype. Her story speaks to universal truths about life and spirituality, reminding us that the divine feminine is not a static ideal but a dynamic force that holds space for grief, love, and the endless cycles of transformation.

Through her connection to the Black Madonna, Isis offers a lens to see the sacred in all aspects of existence: the light and the dark, the sorrow and the joy, the endings and the beginnings. As you reflect on her story and influence, may you find the courage to embrace your journey of transformation, just as Isis did, and carry her wisdom into your daily life.

THE ETHIOPIAN BLACK MADONNA

In the rugged highlands of Ethiopia, a land steeped in ancient spirituality and deep Christian roots, the Black Madonna holds a place of profound reverence. Known as *Kidist Mariam* (Holy Mary), the Ethiopian Black Madonna is more than an icon—she is a sacred presence woven into the fabric of Ethiopian Christianity. Her dark features, a reflection of the local population's skin tone, not only mirror their cultural identity but also symbolize the universality of the divine feminine within this unique and deeply spiritual tradition.

The Unique Devotion To Mary In Ethiopian Christianity

Ethiopia's Christian heritage dates back to the 4th century CE, making it one of the earliest nations to adopt Christianity. The Ethiopian Orthodox Tewahedo Church has a rich tradition of Marian devotion, and the Black Madonna plays a central role in the spiritual lives of its followers. Mary is revered not only as the mother of Jesus but also as an intercessor, protector, and a symbol of hope for the faithful, reflecting the depth of spiritual connection in Ethiopian Christianity.

The Ethiopian Black Madonna is often depicted in religious art and icons, characterized by her deep, rich complexion and regal posture. These depictions are not simply artistic choices—they reflect Ethiopia's deep connection to Mary as a mother figure who mirrors their cultural identity and spiritual values. Her image is a powerful affirmation that the divine is present in all people, transcending race and geography.

Her Role As A Protector And Guide

The Ethiopian Black Madonna is often associated with miraculous interventions and divine protection. One of the most famous depictions is found in the Church of St. Mary of Zion in Axum, which is believed to house the Ark of the

Covenant. This sacred site has become a center for Marian devotion, with pilgrims traveling across the country to pray for her guidance and blessings. In Ethiopian spirituality, Mary is a bridge between humanity and the divine. Her protective role is highlighted during times of hardship and conflict. Throughout Ethiopia's history, the Black Madonna was invoked as a guardian of the people when the nation faced invasions and adversities. Her presence offered strength and reassurance that they were not alone in their struggles.

In Ethiopian spirituality, Mary is a bridge between humanity and the divine. Her protective role is highlighted during times of hardship and conflict. Throughout Ethiopia's history, the Black Madonna was invoked as a guardian of the people when the nation faced invasions and adversities. Her presence offered strength and reassurance that they were not alone in their struggles.

Practical Example:

A well-known story tells of Ethiopian soldiers carrying Marian icons into battle during times of war. They believed her presence would protect them and guide them to victory. This deep trust in Mary's power as a protector continues today as people turn to the Ethiopian Black Madonna for comfort and strength in personal and communal challenges.

The Symbolism Of Her Darkness

The Ethiopian Black Madonna's dark features reflect her cultural context and symbolize her spiritual essence. Her darkness carries profound meaning—it symbolizes mystery, depth, and the fertile ground of creation.

In Ethiopian Christianity, darkness is not feared but embraced as part of the divine mystery. The Black Madonna's complexion reminds us that the sacred is not confined to light or purity but also exists in the richness of life's complexities. Her image encourages her followers to embrace their own struggles and see the divine in all aspects of their lives, even in times of uncertainty.

Practical Lessons From The Ethiopian Black Madonna

The Ethiopian Black Madonna offers profound spiritual lessons deeply rooted in tradition and universally relevant.

Practical Advice:

1. **Call on Her for Protection:** In moments of fear or uncertainty, turn to the Ethiopian Black Madonna as a source of strength. Light a candle and ask for her guidance, envisioning her as a nurturing force that shields and supports you.

2. **Embrace Your Unique Identity:** Like the Ethiopian Black Madonna, celebrate the aspects of yourself that make you unique. Reflect on how your heritage, culture, or personal experiences shape your spiritual journey.

3. **Find the Sacred in the Struggle:** When facing challenges, remember the Black Madonna's role as a symbol of resilience. Journal about a difficult time and how it helped you grow. Let her story remind you that strength is born from hardship.

A Timeless Presence In Ethiopian Spirituality

The Ethiopian Black Madonna is a testament to the enduring power of the divine feminine. Her role in Ethiopian Christianity transcends mere iconography—she is a living symbol of hope, protection, and cultural pride. The Ethiopian people have found strength in their faith and a deep connection to the sacred feminine through her.

For those seeking to understand the Black Madonna's role on a global scale, the Ethiopian tradition offers a powerful example of how the sacred feminine can serve as both a spiritual and cultural anchor. Her presence calls us to honor our roots, embrace life's complexities, and trust the divine wisdom that guides us all.

THE BLACK MADONNA'S HIDDEN PRESENCE IN MIDDLE EASTERN TRADITIONS

The Middle East, often considered the cradle of civilization, has long been a melting pot of spiritual beliefs, cultural exchanges, and religious evolution. While the Black Madonna is not as openly recognized in Middle Eastern traditions as in other parts of the world, her archetype is deeply rooted in the region's ancient goddesses and later integrated into Abrahamic religions. Her hidden presence can be traced back to powerful feminine deities like Astarte and Ishtar, whose qualities resonate with the essence of the Black Madonna.

Links to Goddesses like Astarte

Astarte, the ancient Canaanite goddess of fertility, love, and war, is one of the most profound precursors to the Black

Madonna archetype in the Middle East. Often depicted as a maternal figure yet fierce and commanding, Astarte embodies the duality of creation and destruction, love and power—qualities mirrored in the Black Madonna's symbolism.

Astarte was worshipped across the Levant, particularly in Phoenician and Canaanite cultures. Her temples often featured sacred altars where devotees sought her blessings for fertility, protection, and success in battle. As the Middle East transitioned into monotheistic traditions, worshipping goddesses like Astarte was suppressed or absorbed into newer religious frameworks. However, the divine feminine archetype persisted, reemerging in different forms.

With her dark, enigmatic visage, the Black Madonna carries forward the mystery and power associated with Astarte. Just as Astarte was revered as a source of life and protector of the vulnerable, the Black Madonna embodies these same qualities as a universal mother figure.

Practical Lesson:

Astarte's legacy reminds us to embrace our duality—the ability to nurture and protect while standing firm in our strength. Reflect on moments in your life when you've balanced these qualities. How can you honor your softer and more assertive sides daily?

The Influence Of Ishtar And Inanna

The Black Madonna archetype also shares a lineage with Ishtar (and her earlier Sumerian counterpart, Inanna), the goddess of love, fertility, and the underworld. Ishtar's descent into the underworld—a journey of surrender, transformation, and eventual rebirth—parallels the spiritual themes embodied by the Black Madonna.

Ishtar's dark journey symbolizes the need to confront the shadow self, a theme central to the Black Madonna's energy. In Middle Eastern traditions, Ishtar's association with the stars and the heavens highlights her connection to cosmic cycles, fertility, and life's inherent mysteries.

As Abrahamic religions developed, Ishtar's qualities were absorbed and reinterpreted, influencing Marian devotion in Christianity and some mystical interpretations within Islam. As a result, the Black Madonna carries the echoes of Ishtar's transformative power and her role as a guide through life's darkest moments.

Practical Lesson:

Use Ishtar's descent as a model for your spiritual growth. When faced with challenges, remember that surrendering to the process is often the first step toward transformation. Journal about a recent challenge and what it taught you about yourself.

Integration Into Abrahamic Religions

The Middle East is home to the Abrahamic religions— Judaism, Christianity, and Islam—all of which have nuanced relationships with the divine feminine. While the figure of Mary, the mother of Jesus, became central in Christian theology, her characteristics often reflect the earlier goddess archetypes of the region.

In Christianity, Mary's nurturing role as the mother of Christ aligns with Astarte's association with fertility and life-giving power. Similarly, Mary's title as *Theotokos* (God-bearer) echoes the divine mother archetype found in Ishtar and other Middle Eastern goddesses. The Black Madonna, with her darker complexion and mysterious aura, represents a continuation of this sacred lineage, blending the goddess traditions with Christian devotion.

In Islam, Mary (*Maryam*) is venerated as one of the most important women in the Qur'an. Her qualities of purity, strength, and divine favor resonate with the archetype of the divine feminine. Although Islam does not depict Mary visually, reverence for her transcends cultural and geographic boundaries.

The Black Madonna's hidden presence in these traditions reminds us that the sacred feminine cannot be erased—it simply takes on new forms and continues to guide humanity through its ever-evolving spiritual journey.

Practical Ways To Honor The Middle Eastern Divine Feminine

The hidden threads of the Black Madonna in Middle Eastern traditions invite us to reflect on the universal presence of the sacred feminine. Here are some ways to connect with her energy:

1. **Embrace Cycles of Transformation:** Use Ishtar's descent as inspiration to accept life's cycles of loss and renewal. During times of change, remind yourself that every descent into difficulty holds growth potential.

2. **Create a Sacred Space:** Set up a small altar with

3. symbols of the divine feminine, such as a candle, a bowl of water, or a flower. Use this space to meditate or reflect on the qualities of Astarte, Ishtar, or Mary.

4. **Honor Your Strength and Nurturing Qualities:** Just as the Black Madonna holds space for protection and compassion, journal how you can embody these dual qualities in your own life.

The Timeless Feminine Presence In The Middle East

The Black Madonna's hidden presence in Middle Eastern traditions reveals a profound truth: the sacred feminine is eternal. Though the forms and names may change—Astarte, Ishtar, Mary—her essence remains. She is the mother who nurtures, the warrior who protects, and the guide who leads us through life's mysteries.

Exploring these ancient roots reminds us that the Black Madonna is not confined to a single region or tradition. She transcends time and culture, inviting us to embrace her wisdom in our lives and spiritual practices. Through her, we see that the divine feminine is not separate from us—it lives within, waiting to be rediscovered.

4: THE BLACK MADONNA IN THE AMERICAS

"In the shadow of the Black Madonna, we find not darkness, but the deep, sacred wellspring of life and creation."

HER JOURNEY ACROSS THE ATLANTIC

OUR LADY OF GUADALUPE

Among the most famous and beloved depictions of the Black Madonna in the Americas is *Our Lady of Guadalupe,* who holds a central place in the heart of Mexican spirituality. Revered as a protector, mother, and unifier, she is far more than a religious icon—she is a bridge between indigenous traditions and Christian beliefs, symbolizing a fusion of faiths and cultures.

How Indigenous And Christian Beliefs Merged In Mexico

The story of Our Lady of Guadalupe begins in 1531, a decade after the Spanish conquest of the Aztec Empire. According to tradition, she appeared to an indigenous man named Juan Diego on the hill of Tepeyac, which had long been a sacred site dedicated to the Aztec goddess Tonantzin, the mother deity associated with fertility and the earth.

Draped in a cloak of stars and speaking in Nahuatl, the language of the Aztec people, Our Lady of Guadalupe asked Juan Diego to build a church in her honor. When the skeptical bishop demanded proof of her appearance, she instructed Juan Diego to gather roses from the barren, wintry hillside. He placed the flowers in his tilma (cloak), and when he unfurled it before the bishop, her miraculous image was imprinted on the fabric.

This merging of the Christian Mary with Tonantzin reflects indigenous and Catholic traditions synthesis. For the native people, Our Lady of Guadalupe represented continuity with their ancestral spiritual practices while embodying the Christian faith imposed by the Spanish colonizers. Her dark skin and use of Nahuatl further signified her connection to the indigenous population, affirming their dignity and worth during oppression and upheaval.

Her Role As A Unifier And Protector

Our Lady of Guadalupe is often referred to as the *Mother of Mexico*. She is seen as a protector of the poor, the oppressed, and the marginalized. In her image, she holds a quiet power— her dark complexion and humble yet regal posture remind people that the divine is accessible to all, regardless of social status or ethnicity.

Her protective role has been evident throughout Mexican history. During the fight for independence in the early 19th century, revolutionary leaders like Miguel Hidalgo invoked her as a symbol of unity and resistance. She has continued to serve as a source of hope and strength for generations, especially for women, indigenous communities, and immigrants seeking solace and guidance.

Practical Example:

A migrant family traveling north searching for a better life might carry a small image of Our Lady of Guadalupe in their pocket or bag. She is not just a figure of faith but a reminder that they are protected, loved, and guided, even in the most uncertain and challenging moments.

The Symbolism Of Our Lady Of Guadalupe

Imprinted on Juan Diego's tilma, her image is rich with symbolic meaning. She stands on a crescent moon, a nod to Tonantzin and the earth's cycles, while her blue-green mantle adorned with stars evokes the heavens. Her posture is humble, hands clasped in prayer, yet her gaze is steady and confident, a reminder of her divine authority.

The Black Madonna's essence shines through in Our Lady of Guadalupe's duality—her ability to hold light and shadow, indigenous and Christian, heaven and earth. This duality makes her relatable to many people as she bridges the gaps between faiths, cultures, and personal struggles.

Practical Advice:

Practical Advice: spend time reflecting on the image of Our Lady of Guadalupe. Notice the balance in her symbolism—earthly and heavenly, humble yet powerful. Consider how you can embody a similar balance in your life, honoring your roots while growing into new expressions of yourself. This reflection can empower you to navigate personal challenges and foster personal growth.

Modern Devotion And Feminine Empowerment

For many women, Our Lady of Guadalupe is more than a religious figure. She represents the strength and resilience of the feminine spirit. She is a symbol of empowerment, reminding us that femininity is not just nurturing and gentle but also fierce, courageous, and unyielding. Women across the Americas turn to her in times of personal struggle, finding in her an ally and advocate who understands the complexities of their lives.

Her annual feast day, December 12, is a testament to her enduring presence as a source of inspiration, healing, and unity. It brings millions of pilgrims to the Basilica of Our Lady of Guadalupe in Mexico City, where people walk for miles, often barefoot, to honor her and give thanks for her blessings. This devotion is a living tradition that continues to inspire and unite people across the Americas.

Practical Example:

Celebrate your strength and resilience by honoring Our Lady of Guadalupe in a personal ritual. Light a candle, offer a flower, and reflect on a moment you overcame adversity. Invite her energy to guide you through any challenges you may face.

A Bridge Between Worlds

Our Lady of Guadalupe is a powerful symbol of unity and transformation. She bridges the divide between indigenous traditions and Christianity, between light and shadow, and between the earthly and the divine. Through her presence, she invites us to embrace our full selves—our history, our struggles, and our potential to grow into something greater.

As a Black Madonna of the Americas, she reminds us that divinity is not exclusive or distant but is present in every culture, every struggle, and every person. Connecting with her reminds us to honor our roots, celebrate our resilience, and find strength in the balance of who we are and who we are becoming.

OUR LADY OF APARECIDA

In Brazil, *Nossa Senhora Aparecida*—Our Lady of Aparecida—holds a profound place in the hearts of millions. She is not only a cherished Catholic figure but also a symbol of resilience and hope and a reflection of the nation's diverse cultural identity. Her origins, wrapped in legend and faith, offer a compelling narrative that continues to inspire and empower generations.

The story of Our Lady of Aparecida begins in 1717 along the Paraíba River in São Paulo. Local fishermen, tasked with providing fish for a governor's banquet, struggled with empty nets. Facing failure, they cast their nets one final time and pulled up the headless clay figure of a statue. Undeterred, they cast again, retrieving the missing head. Shortly after, their nets overflowed with fish—a moment interpreted as a divine intervention.

With its dark complexion and humble origins, this clay statue became a focal point of devotion. It wasn't long before stories of miracles attributed to her began circulating, drawing pilgrims to venerate her. What started as a small act of faith by a few fishermen grew into a movement that shaped Brazilian spirituality, transcending religious boundaries and symbolizing hope for the oppressed and marginalized.

Cultural And Spiritual Significance

Our Lady of Aparecida's dark complexion is vital to her identity, profoundly resonating with Brazil's Afro-descendant and indigenous populations. In a nation marked by the legacy of colonization and slavery, she stands as an inclusive representation of divinity, offering a source of empowerment to those historically excluded from mainstream spiritual narratives.

Her presence carries a dual significance. Spiritually, she embodies the maternal qualities of love, protection, and intercession. Culturally, she serves as a symbol of unity in a country rich with racial and ethnic diversity. For many, she represents the ability to find strength and grace amid adversity.

Every October 12, millions of devotees journey to the Basilica of Our Lady of Aparecida in São Paulo. This pilgrimage is a profound act of devotion, often involving walking great distances, praying the Rosary, or carrying replicas of the statue. These acts, undertaken by people of all ages and backgrounds, reflect a collective yearning for connection, healing, and transformation.

Practical Lessons From Her Story

The story of Our Lady of Aparecida carries timeless lessons that extend beyond her miraculous origins, offering guidance for those navigating life's challenges.

Faith Amid Adversity

1. The fishermen's perseverance in facing failure is a testament to faith and determination. Even when their nets were empty, they continued trying, ultimately finding fish and a profound symbol of hope.

Practical advice: When facing difficulties, focus on consistent effort, even if immediate results seem unlikely. Trust that persistence often leads to unexpected blessings, even when the path forward feels uncertain.

The Power Of Representation

1. Our Lady of Aparecida's dark skin has resonated with communities often excluded from depictions of the divine. Her image challenges traditional norms and emphasizes the inclusivity of spirituality.

Practical advice: Engage in practices that celebrate diversity. Whether exploring spiritual traditions outside your own or creating spaces where all voices are heard, inclusivity deepens personal and collective growth.

Strength Through Community

1. Devotion to Our Lady of Aparecida is deeply communal. Her story demonstrates the transformative power of coming together in faith and purpose, from shared prayers to collective pilgrimages.

Practical advice: Seek out or create supportive spiritual communities. Whether it's a women's circle, a meditation group, or a prayer gathering, shared experiences can amplify personal transformation and healing.

Real-World Applications

Our Lady of Aparecida's legacy continues to inspire movements for social justice. Afro-Brazilian and Indigenous communities often invoke her as a symbol of resilience in the face of systemic inequality. Her image is carried during protests, a reminder that spirituality and activism are deeply intertwined.

Her story also resonates strongly with advocates for feminine empowerment. Our Lady of Aparecida embodies compassion, strength, and perseverance, reminding women of their ability to navigate challenges gracefully. In a world where expectations often pull women in multiple directions, she offers a model for balancing strength and nurturing.

Practical advice: Reflect on the ways resilience has shaped your journey. Identify moments when you've drawn upon inner strength to overcome challenges. Use these reflections to empower yourself or inspire others toward growth and healing.

AFRICAN DIASPORA AND THE BLACK MADONNA

Influence Of African Spirituality On Black Madonna Figures In The Caribbean And South America

The transatlantic slave trade uprooted millions of Africans, carrying their cultures, beliefs, and traditions to the Americas. Despite the brutal conditions of slavery, these spiritual practices survived, adapted, and fused with the dominant Catholicism of colonial powers, giving rise to unique expressions of faith. The Black Madonna emerged as a profound symbol of this syncretism, embodying African spiritual traditions and the Marian devotion introduced by European colonizers.

In the Caribbean and South America, the Black Madonna became more than a Catholic figure; she evolved into a bridge between African ancestral wisdom and Christian iconography. Her dark complexion, often interpreted as an acknowledgment of African heritage, allowed enslaved and oppressed peoples to see themselves reflected in the divine— this merging of traditions created rich, multilayered expressions of spirituality that continue to thrive today.

The Caribbean: Syncretism And Survival

In the Caribbean, particularly Haiti, Cuba, and the Dominican Republic, the Black Madonna became intertwined with African-derived spiritual systems such as Vodou, Santería, and Candomblé. These traditions preserved elements of Yoruba, Fon, and other West African religions, adapting them to the new cultural and religious environment of the Americas.

In Haiti, for example, the Black Madonna is often syncretized with *Erzulie Dantor*, a powerful *law* (spirit) associated with love, protection, and motherhood in Vodou. Depictions of *Erzulie Dantor* usually feature dark-skinned icons of the Virgin Mary, especially the image of Our Lady of Czestochowa, another renowned Black Madonna figure. Enslaved Haitians, forbidden from openly practicing their ancestral religions, found ways to worship their spirits under the guise of Catholic saints. This blending allowed the Black Madonna to serve as a figure of spiritual devotion and a source of cultural and personal empowerment.

Similarly, the Black Madonna is venerated in Cuba through *La Virgen de la Caridad del Cobre* (Our Lady of Charity of El Cobre). She is a Catholic symbol representing *Ochún*, the Yoruba orisha of love, fertility, and rivers. This duality allowed enslaved Africans to maintain their connection to Ochún while outwardly adhering to Catholicism. The Black Madonna's role as a nurturing, protective figure aligns with Ochún's qualities, reinforcing her significance in the spiritual lives of Afro-Cubans.

South America: The Black Madonna In Afro-Brazilian Traditions

In Brazil, the legacy of African spirituality is deeply embedded in the country's culture, mainly through Candomblé and Umbanda. These Afro-Brazilian religions emphasize the worship of orishas and spirits, often syncretized with Catholic saints and figures, including the Black Madonna.

The figure of Our Lady of Aparecida, Brazil's patroness, carries strong echoes of African influence. While officially a Catholic symbol, she is revered within Afro-Brazilian traditions as embodying qualities of orishas such as *Yemanjá* and *Nanã*, both maternal and protective forces in African spirituality. This reverence reflects the resilience of African cultural traditions, which persist despite centuries of oppression.

In Salvador, Bahia—a city often called the spiritual heart of Afro-Brazilian culture—Our Lady of Aparecida is celebrated with vibrant processions that merge Catholic rituals with African drumming, singing, and dance. These festivities are not only acts of devotion but also affirmations of cultural identity and resistance. For many, the Black Madonna represents both the divine and the ancestral, a reminder of the strength and creativity that have sustained their communities through generations of struggle.

Practical Lessons From The Diaspora's Influence

Integrating African spirituality with Marian devotion reveals the transformative power of adaptation and resilience. These traditions offer valuable insights for those seeking spiritual empowerment or navigating personal challenges.

Honoring Ancestry In Spiritual Practice

1. Syncretism in the diaspora demonstrates the importance of honoring one's roots while embracing new forms of expression. The Black Madonna's role as a

bridge between African traditions and Catholicism is a powerful example of how spirituality can evolve without losing its essence.

Practical advice: Explore your spiritual lineage, whether through cultural traditions, ancestral practices, or modern adaptations. Allow this exploration to deepen your connection to your spiritual path while remaining open to growth and new influences.

Strength In Adaptation

1. The survival of African spirituality within the framework of Catholicism highlights the ability to adapt and thrive even under oppressive conditions. This adaptability reminds us of our inner strength.

Practical advice: Reflect on areas where you've had to adapt to difficult circumstances. What resources, internal or external, helped you navigate those challenges? Incorporate these lessons into your spiritual practices to cultivate resilience.

Embodying Duality

1. The Black Madonna's dual role as a Catholic icon and a vessel for African spiritual forces teaches us that duality can be a power source. Spirituality need not be rigid or confined to one tradition—it can be fluid and multi-faceted.

Practical advice: Embrace the dualities within yourself. If you feel pulled between different spiritual traditions, practices, or beliefs, allow them to coexist. Journaling or meditating on how these aspects intersect can offer clarity and empowerment.

Real-World Applications

The influence of African spirituality on the Black Madonna continues to be a source of cultural pride and spiritual renewal. In modern-day Haiti, Cuba, and Brazil, festivals, rituals, and ceremonies honoring the Black Madonna are not only acts of worship but also celebrations of heritage and identity. These events serve as reminders of the enduring legacy of the African diaspora, offering opportunities for connection, reflection, and healing.

For feminine empowerment advocates, the Black Madonna represents the blending of strength and nurturing, spiritual power, and cultural pride. Her duality challenges traditional notions of femininity, encouraging women to embrace their full complexity and draw strength from their heritage.

Practical advice: Engage with cultural or spiritual practices that honor your individuality and connection to a larger community. Whether through dance, storytelling, or ceremony, these practices can deepen your understanding of self and foster a sense of belonging.

5: THE MYTHS AND MYSTERIES OF THE BLACK MADONNA

"She is the silent protector, the dark mother who holds both the light and the shadow, guiding us through the unseen realms."

HIDDEN STORIES AND SYMBOLS

LEGENDS SURROUNDING THE BLACK MADONNA

Across cultures and continents, the Black Madonna has been surrounded by an aura of mystique. Her presence evokes reverence and curiosity, inspiring countless legends, miraculous stories, and folk traditions attempting to explain her origins and powers. These tales passed down through generations, reflect the unique cultural, spiritual, and historical contexts in which the Black Madonna is venerated.

The Miraculous Origins Of The Black Madonna

One recurring motif in the legends of the Black Madonna is her mysterious and miraculous discovery. Whether unearthed from the earth, found floating in rivers, or emerging unharmed from fires, these stories speak to the idea that her presence is divinely ordained.

In Poland, the Black Madonna of Częstochowa is said to have been painted by St. Luke on a cedar wood panel from the table of the Holy Family. While scholars debate the historical accuracy of this claim, the legend endures as part of her sacred narrative. According to one popular tale, the painting was brought to Poland from the Byzantine Empire and later hidden to protect it from invading armies. When rediscovered, the image was seen as a sign of divine intervention, solidifying her role as a protector of the Polish people.

In Montserrat, Spain, the Black Madonna of Montserrat—*La Moreneta*—was said to have been discovered by shepherds in a cave after seeing a mysterious light. When attempts were made to move the statue, it became impossibly heavy, a sign that she wished to remain there. This legend ties the Black Madonna to the natural world, portraying her as a guardian of sacred spaces.

Similarly, the Black Madonna of Rocamadour in France was believed to have been carved by St. Amadour, who chose her location as a place of divine retreat. Her miracles drew pilgrims from all over Europe, cementing her as a figure of hope and healing.

Miracles Of Healing And Protection

The Black Madonna is often associated with miraculous healings and acts of protection. Many legends highlight her intercession during times of crisis, be it illness, war, or natural disaster. Her role as a protector and healer resonates with those seeking comfort and strength in their darkest moments.

One of the most famous stories comes from Spain, where *La Virgen de Guadalupe de Extremadura* is credited with saving her devotees during a plague. Farmers and villagers would pray to her, and in many accounts, the sickness would subside or vanish altogether. This association with healing has made her a patroness for those suffering physical and emotional ailments.

In Poland, the Black Madonna of Częstochowa is credited with saving the Jasna Góra Monastery from Swedish invaders during the 17th century. According to legend, when the monastery came under siege, the image of the Black Madonna miraculously repelled the attackers, preserving the site's sanctity. To this day, she is regarded as a symbol of resistance and hope in the face of oppression.

In Latin America, stories abound of Black Madonnas protecting vulnerable populations. For example, Our Lady of Aparecida in Brazil is credited with safeguarding fishermen, farmers, and the poor. Her association with miraculous interventions has elevated her as a maternal figure who stands with those who suffer.

Folk Tales Rooted In Local Traditions

In addition to grand miracles, many Black Madonna legends are rooted in local folklore, blending Christian and pre-Christian beliefs. In these tales, the Black Madonna often appears as a mediator between the human and the divine, offering guidance, wisdom, or assistance, making us feel supported and guided.

In Italy, the Black Madonna of Tindari is said to have caused a shipwreck when sailors stole her image. The locals recovered the statue and enshrined her in a sanctuary overlooking the sea. This story emphasizes her sacred power, connection to nature, and role as a protector of the land and its people.

In some regions, legends tie the Black Madonna to the cycles of the earth and the feminine divine. For instance, her dark complexion is sometimes interpreted as a link to the fertile soil, the womb of the world, and the mysteries of creation. This interpretation varies across cultures, with some seeing her darkness as a symbol of the unknown and others as a representation of the nurturing aspects of the earth. These stories reflect the syncretic blending of Marian devotion with older, earth-based spiritual practices.

Practical Lessons From Legends

The stories surrounding the Black Madonna carry spiritual and symbolic meaning that transcends their folkloric roots. They remind us of universal themes of faith, resilience, and divine feminine power.

Embrace The Mystery

1. The mysterious nature of the Black Madonna invites us to embrace the unknown and trust in the unseen forces that guide us. Legends of her miraculous discoveries and interventions remind us that life often unfolds in ways we cannot predict or control.

Practical Advice: Practice surrendering to life's mysteries.

Whether through meditation, prayer, or reflection, cultivate trust in the process, even when the path is unclear. This could involve setting aside a specific time each day for contemplation, or engaging in a spiritual practice that encourages trust and surrender.

Honor The Sacred In Nature

1. Many legends tie the Black Madonna to natural elements such as caves, rivers, and mountains. These connections invite us to see the divine in the natural world and honor its sacredness.

Practical Advice: Spend time in nature to connect with its rhythms and energy. Create small rituals to express gratitude for the earth, such as lighting a candle or offering flowers at a favorite outdoor spot.

Seek Strength In Community

1. The miraculous acts of the Black Madonna often occur in the context of collective faith, whether during a siege, a plague, or a communal pilgrimage. Her stories remind us of the power of coming together in shared belief and intention.

Practical advice: Join or create a spiritual community to share stories and traditions. Engage in rituals or practices that strengthen collective bonds and amplify individual growth.

Real-World Examples

Devotion to the Black Madonna continues to thrive in regions where these legends are cherished. Pilgrimages to sites like Jasna Góra in Poland, Montserrat in Spain, and Tindari in Italy draw millions of people seeking healing, guidance, or simply a sense of belonging. These traditions, which have endured through generations, are a living testament to the enduring power of her myths and symbols, connecting us to a timeless tradition.

In modern spiritual movements, the Black Madonna continues to inspire those exploring the divine feminine and the interplay between myth and spirituality. Her legends remind us that within every story lies a deeper truth waiting to be uncovered, making us feel part of a living tradition.

SYMBOLS OF SHADOW AND LIGHT

Decoding The Symbolism Of Her Dark Skin And The Light, She Represents

With her enigmatic presence, the Black Madonna invites profound contemplation on the duality of shadow and light. Her dark complexion has sparked debates, inspired spiritual insights, and carried deep symbolic significance across cultures. While some interpret her dark skin as a reflection of racial or ethnic identity, others view it as a spiritual metaphor, embodying the mysteries of the divine feminine, transformation, and the interplay of hidden truths and enlightenment.

The Sacredness Of The Shadow

In many spiritual traditions, the shadow symbolizes the unknown, the hidden, and the fertile ground from which transformation emerges. The Black Madonna's dark complexion can be seen as a representation of this sacred shadow—inviting us to embrace the aspects of life and self that are often overlooked or misunderstood.

Her image encourages integrating what is hidden into the light of awareness. In Jungian psychology, the shadow represents the unconscious parts of ourselves, both feared and disowned. The Black Madonna guides us, leading us into the depths of our inner world to confront and ultimately transform these aspects.

In myths and legends, darkness often symbolizes creation. The fertile black soil nurtures life, the womb's darkness gives birth to birth, and the night sky cradles the stars. With her deep, dark presence, the Black Madonna connects us to these archetypal truths, reminding us that creation and renewal often begin in the depths of the unseen.

Light Emerging From The Darkness

Paradoxically, while the Black Madonna is a figure of shadow, she is equally a bearer of light. Across traditions, she is often associated with miracles, healing, and guidance—qualities that symbolize divine illumination. The juxtaposition of her dark skin with the light she embodies mirrors the spiritual journey of transformation, where navigating life's challenges leads to wisdom and enlightenment.

For example, in the legend of the Black Madonna of

Montserrat, the cave where she was discovered represents the dark, mysterious space of the unknown. Yet, her emergence from this cave into the light signifies revelation and hope. This interplay between shadow and light teaches us that profound clarity and purpose can come from the depths of struggle and uncertainty.

In Christian mysticism, the Black Madonna is sometimes seen as embodying Mary's suffering and endurance during Christ's Passion. Her dark complexion symbolizes her connection to human pain, while her ability to provide comfort and guidance reflects the redemptive power of divine love. She bridges the gap between human frailty and divine strength, offering solace to those who seek her intercession.

The Alchemical Nature Of Transformation

The Black Madonna's symbolism aligns with alchemical traditions, where the black phase (*nigredo*) marks the beginning of the transformation process. In alchemy, the *nigredo* is the stage where the old self is broken down, impurities are burned away, and the soul is prepared for rebirth.

The Black Madonna, with her dark complexion, embodies this transformative process. She invites spiritual seekers to confront the darkness within, not as a source of fear but as a necessary step toward growth and illumination. Her presence reminds us that light and shadow are not opposites but complementary forces that work together to bring about wholeness.

Practical Lessons From Her Symbolism

The Black Madonna's symbolism of shadow and light

provides timeless lessons for those seeking to deepen their spiritual journey and navigate the complexities of life.

Embrace The Shadow

1. The Black Madonna's dark complexion encourages us to explore and integrate the parts of ourselves we may avoid or suppress. These aspects, though uncomfortable, often hold the key to personal growth and healing.

Practical Advice: Take time for self-reflection. Journaling, meditation, or therapist work can help you identify and integrate your shadow aspects. Look at challenges as opportunities for self-discovery rather than obstacles to avoid.

Seek The Light In The Darkness

1. Her light emerges not despite her darkness but through it. This teaches us to find meaning and hope even in life's most challenging moments.

Practical Advice: When faced with difficulties, focus on the lessons they offer. Create rituals that honor your struggles and progress, such as lighting a candle during a reflective moment or expressing gratitude for small victories.

Honor The Cycles Of Transformation

1. Just as the Black Madonna embodies the alchemical process of change, our own lives move through cycles

of darkness and light. Acknowledging these cycles allows us to navigate them with grace.

Practical Advice: Pay attention to your life's natural rhythms. Embrace periods of rest and reflection as opportunities for renewal. Consider setting intentions or affirmations during significant life transitions to anchor your transformation process.

Real-World Applications

The Black Madonna's dual symbolism of shadow and light resonates with modern seekers. In art, literature, and spiritual practices, she symbolizes empowerment for those navigating identity, adversity, or transformation. Feminine empowerment movements often draw on her image, celebrating the strength and beauty of embracing the full spectrum of human experience.

For instance, spiritual retreats focused on the Black Madonna often incorporate shadow work—practices that guide participants in confronting and healing unresolved emotional or spiritual wounds. These retreats draw on her symbolism to create safe spaces for self-exploration, offering participants a chance to emerge more substantial and whole.

In community rituals and celebrations, particularly in regions where the Black Madonna is revered, her image reminds participants of the shared experience of human struggle and triumph. Whether through candlelit processions, music, or storytelling, these practices honor the cycles of darkness and light that define our lives.

Practical Advice: Look to the Black Madonna as a source of inspiration for your spiritual practices. Incorporate symbols of light and shadow into your rituals, such as dark stones or candles, to remind yourself of the beauty and wisdom that arise from integrating both aspects. Let her image guide you toward a deeper understanding of your transformative journey.

HER ROLE AS A BRIDGE BETWEEN TRADITIONS

The Black Madonna stands at the crossroads of ancient goddess worship and Christian devotion, embodying qualities that resonate across spiritual traditions. Her presence reflects a lineage of feminine divinity that predates Christianity, making her a continuation of and a departure from the sacred feminine archetypes celebrated in pre-Christian times. As a bridge between traditions, the Black Madonna represents the integration of old and new, uniting the mysticism of ancient goddesses with the maternal, intercessory role of the Virgin Mary in Christianity.

Echoes Of Ancient Goddess Worship

Before the rise of Christianity, goddess worship was central to spiritual life in many cultures. Goddesses such as Isis in Egypt, Cybele in Anatolia, Demeter in Greece, and Inanna in Mesopotamia symbolized fertility, creation, destruction, and transformation. They represented the cyclical rhythms of nature, the sacredness of the earth, and the mysteries of birth and death. These goddesses were often depicted with dark or black features, emphasizing their connection to the fertile earth and the cosmic void from which all creation emerges.

Isis, for example, was an influential mother figure in Egyptian mythology, known for her magical abilities and role in resurrecting her husband, Osiris. Her iconography—often showing her nursing her son, Horus—parallels later Christian depictions of the Virgin Mary with the Christ child. When the worship of Isis spread throughout the Roman Empire, her attributes began to merge with emerging Marian devotion. Scholars believe that early Christians may have adopted elements of Isis worship to ease the transition for converts, allowing familiar images and rituals to take on new meanings.

Similarly, in Greco-Roman traditions, the Great Mother Cybele was honored as a protector and a nurturer, particularly of the downtrodden. Her cult often centered on caves, mountains, and other sacred natural sites—settings later associated with many Black Madonna shrines. The dark-skinned depictions of Cybele in some regions underscore her connection to the earth and the mysteries of life and death. These visual and thematic elements likely influenced how the Black Madonna was conceived and venerated in Christian contexts.

The Virgin Mary As A Transformative Archetype

With the rise of Christianity, devotion to the Virgin Mary became a focal point of spiritual practice, but traces of ancient goddess worship remained. The Black Madonna, in particular, retains qualities associated with the divine feminine archetypes of earlier traditions. Her dark complexion, connection to nature, and reputation for miraculous intercession align her with goddesses who embodied the mysteries of creation and transformation.

The Black Madonna served as a symbolic bridge in the transition from goddess worship to Marian devotion. For example, in regions where devotion to goddesses like Isis, Artemis, or Demeter was intense, Black Madonna figures often emerged at former pagan worship sites. Many of these sites, such as caves, springs, or mountains, carried deep spiritual significance and were reimagined as places of Marian devotion.

One example is the Black Madonna of Montserrat in Spain, whose shrine is in the mountains. This location echoes ancient practices of honoring earth goddesses in elevated or secluded spaces. Similarly, the Black Madonna of Rocamadour in France resides in a cave, a site long associated with the womb-like symbolism of the earth and the nurturing aspects of the divine feminine.

Syncretism And Spiritual Adaptation

The Black Madonna's enduring presence reveals how spiritual traditions adapt and merge over time. Rather than erasing the goddess traditions that came before, Christianity—consciously or unconsciously—absorbed elements of those practices into Marian devotion. This syncretism allowed communities to maintain their connection to the sacred feminine while embracing a new spiritual framework.

In some cases, the integration was intentional. Early Christian missionaries often repurposed pagan symbols and sites to facilitate conversion. By incorporating familiar imagery, such as the nurturing mother figure, the transition to Christianity became more seamless for those steeped in goddess worship. With her maternal qualities and mysterious presence, the Black Madonna embodied this continuity while also introducing the redemptive themes central to Christianity.

In other instances, the adaptation was organic, born from the collective unconscious of communities that continued to revere the sacred feminine. This unbroken thread between goddess worship and the Black Madonna illustrates humanity's enduring need to honor the divine in feminine form—recognizing the balance between creation and destruction, light and shadow, nurturing and power.

Practical Lessons From The Black Madonna's Role

The Black Madonna's ability to bridge traditions offers profound insights for those seeking spiritual growth in a complex, interconnected world.

Embrace Spiritual Syncretism

1. The Black Madonna demonstrates that spiritual traditions are not rigid or exclusive but fluid and evolving. She embodies the wisdom of honoring the old and the new, creating a space where diverse practices coexist.

Practical Advice: Explore the intersections of different spiritual traditions. Study their shared symbols, values, and archetypes to deepen your understanding of the sacred. This approach can foster a more inclusive and expansive spiritual practice.

Honor The Feminine Archetype

1. The Black Madonna represents the divine feminine in its many forms—nurturer, protector, and transformer. By honoring these qualities, we can experience a deeper sense of balance and creativity in our lives.

Practical Advice: Create rituals or meditative practices that celebrate the divine feminine. Through art, prayer, or movement, allow yourself to embody qualities like compassion, strength, and renewal.

Recognize The Sacred In Transition

1. Just as the Black Madonna emerged as a bridge between traditions, she reminds us that transformation often involves integrating the past with the present. Spiritual growth is not about abandoning what came before but weaving it into a more complete understanding of the divine.

Practical Advice: Reflect on the transitions in your own life. What aspects of your past can be honored and carried forward? How can you integrate old wisdom with new insights to create a fuller sense of self?

Real-World Examples

The Black Madonna continues to inspire scholarly exploration and spiritual practice, particularly among those interested in reclaiming the sacred feminine. Modern devotees often explore her connection to ancient goddess traditions to deepen their understanding of the divine.

For example, feminist theologians and spiritual practitioners have used the Black Madonna as a focal point for rediscovering the feminine aspects of divinity, emphasizing her role as a symbol of empowerment and healing. Participants often draw on her dual heritage in rituals and retreats centered on the Black Madonna, blending ancient symbols with contemporary spiritual practices.

In places like Montserrat, Spain, and Chartres, France, pilgrimages to Black Madonna shrines continue to attract those seeking a deeper connection to their spiritual roots. These sites serve as reminders of the Black Madonna's ability to unite seemingly disparate traditions, offering a space for contemplation, renewal, and the honoring of life's mysteries.

Practical Advice: If possible, visit a site associated with the Black Madonna to experience her symbolic resonance firsthand. Alternatively, create your own sacred space at home by incorporating symbols of the feminine divine, such as candles, flowers, or images of the Black Madonna, to honor the interconnectedness of spiritual traditions.

6: THE BLACK MADONNA AND THE SHADOW SELF

"Her myths stretch across continents, cultures, and centuries, yet her message remains the same: love, protection, strength, and transformation."

A GUIDE TO EMBRACING THE SHADOW

THE SYMBOLISM OF DARKNESS IN SPIRITUALITY

How Darkness Represents The Unknown And Unhealed Parts Of Ourselves

In spirituality, darkness has long been a powerful symbol of mystery, transformation, and self-discovery. Often misunderstood as something to be feared or avoided, darkness instead offers a sacred invitation to journey inward. It represents our unknown and unhealed parts—the aspects we hide, suppress, or fail to acknowledge. With her dark complexion and enigmatic presence, the Black Madonna embodies this symbolism, serving as a compassionate guide through the shadows of our inner world.

Darkness As The Fertile Ground Of Transformation

In nature, the most prosperous growth often occurs in the dark. Seeds take root in the soil, gestating unseen before breaking through the surface. Nightfall brings rest and restoration, allowing the body and spirit to renew. Similarly, the spiritual darkness represented by the shadow self is not a place of despair but of fertile potential.

The shadow self, a concept popularized by Carl Jung, consists of the unconscious parts of ourselves that we deny or reject. These aspects often stem from fears, insecurities, or societal conditioning. For example, a person taught that vulnerability is a weakness may repress their need for emotional connection, creating a shadow aspect that influences their relationships.

Through her connection to darkness, the Black Madonna invites us to acknowledge these hidden parts of ourselves. She teaches that the shadow is not an enemy but a companion on the path to wholeness. Her presence encourages us to delve into the unknown with courage and compassion, trusting that the process of self-exploration will yield growth and healing.

Darkness As A Space Of Mystery And Potential

The spiritual symbolism of darkness also aligns with mystery and the sacred unknown. Just as the Black Madonna's dark complexion evokes reverence and intrigue, the darkness within us holds truths waiting to be uncovered. It is in the unlit spaces of our consciousness that we encounter our deepest fears and our most profound wisdom.

Many spiritual traditions emphasize the transformative power of darkness. In Hinduism, with her dark skin and fierce demeanor, the goddess Kali represents destruction and rebirth—dismantling illusions to reveal more profound truths. Similarly, in Christianity, the Holy Saturday vigil symbolizes the waiting period in darkness before the resurrection, highlighting the necessity of embracing uncertainty and trust during transformative times.

The Black Madonna embodies this duality of destruction and creation, inviting us to confront our shadow self not as a way to eradicate it but to integrate it. She reminds us that we can only access the light hidden within by exploring the darkness.

The Healing Process Of Confronting The Shadow

Confronting the unknown and unhealed parts of ourselves is not a simple or linear process. It requires patience, courage, and self-compassion. The shadow often manifests through projections, triggers, or recurring patterns that we may find difficult to face. For example, feelings of jealousy, anger, or inadequacy might surface unexpectedly, revealing unmet needs or unresolved wounds.

The Black Madonna guides us during these moments of discomfort. Her maternal energy offers reassurance that the journey inward, while challenging, is a sacred act of self-love. Her nurturing symbolism reminds us that looking into the shadow is not about judgment but about understanding and integration.

Practical Lessons From The Symbolism Of Darkness

The darkness associated with the Black Madonna provides a roadmap for working with the shadow self. Her presence invites us to approach the unknown with reverence and curiosity, turning inward to explore the parts of ourselves we may have ignored or feared.

Learn To Sit With The Unknown

1. The unknown can feel uncomfortable, but it is also where growth begins. The Black Madonna reminds us that true transformation arises when we allow ourselves to sit with uncertainty, trusting the process of self-discovery.

Practical Advice: Practice mindfulness or meditation to build your capacity for stillness and reflection. When uncomfortable emotions arise, resist the urge to distract yourself. Instead, observe them without judgment, acknowledging their presence.

Identify And Embrace Triggers

Triggers often reveal unhealed wounds or hidden beliefs. Rather than avoiding or suppressing them, view them as opportunities for self-awareness and empowerment.

Practical advice: When you notice a strong emotional reaction, pause to explore its origins. Ask yourself, "What part of me feels unseen or unheard right now?" Journaling can help unpack these emotions, offering clarity and insight.

Cultivate Compassion For The Shadow

1. Working with the shadow requires self-compassion. The Black Madonna's nurturing presence reminds us to approach our inner world with kindness rather than criticism.

Practical advice: When reflecting on your shadow self, use affirmations or mantras to cultivate self-compassion. For example: "I honor every part of myself, even the parts I am still learning to love."

Trust In The Transformative Power Of Darkness

1. Just as the Black Madonna's dark skin symbolizes mystery and transformation, the darkness within holds the seeds of renewal. Trust that by confronting your shadow, you are paving the way for greater clarity, peace, and self-understanding.

Practical advice: Create rituals to honor your transformation. For instance, light a candle during moments of reflection to symbolize the light you are bringing into the darkness of your shadow work.

Real-World Applications

The symbolism of darkness has practical implications for modern spiritual seekers. Shadow work has become integral to many healing modalities, from therapy to personal development programs. Retreats dedicated to exploring the divine feminine, particularly those focused on the Black Madonna, often include shadow work as a central component, guiding participants to confront and integrate their inner darkness.

For example, many women's circles or spiritual communities use storytelling, meditation, and creative expression to explore shadow aspects in a supportive environment. These practices reflect the Black Madonna's role as a compassionate guide through the complexities of the shadow self.

In a world that often prioritizes productivity and outward success, the Black Madonna's symbolism serves as a counterbalance, encouraging introspection and inner growth. By embracing our unknown and unhealed parts, we can access deeper truths, break free from limiting patterns, and step into a more authentic and empowered version of ourselves.

THE BLACK MADONNA AS A HEALING ARCHETYPE

Her Role In Confronting Fear, Grief, And Trauma

The Black Madonna is a profound archetype of healing, particularly in relation to fear, grief, and trauma—the often unspoken experiences that shape our inner lives. Her dark and maternal presence offers a sacred container for these emotions, providing comfort and guidance as we navigate the most difficult parts of our personal and collective journeys.

As a healing archetype, the Black Madonna reflects the power of transformation through acknowledgment and integration. By turning toward the shadows of our pain, she shows us how to honor our wounds, embrace our vulnerability, and move through the healing process with compassion and strength.

Confronting Fear

Fear is one of the most pervasive emotions tied to the shadow self. It often arises when we face the unknown, encounter change, or confront parts of ourselves that we have long avoided. The Black Madonna's dark, enigmatic image reminds us that fear is not something to be banished but to be understood.

Her presence calls us to confront fear with courage, not as an act of suppression but as a path to understanding. In this way, the Black Madonna guides us through the uncharted territory of our inner world, helping us discern what lies beneath our fear. Often, fear masks unmet needs, unresolved traumas, or limiting beliefs, and by bringing it into the light of awareness, we can begin to dismantle its power over us.

Practical Advice: When fear arises, pause and reflect. Rather than avoiding or reacting impulsively, ask yourself, "What am I terrified of? What is this fear trying to teach me?" Journaling or discussing these questions with a trusted confidant can help bring clarity and insight.

Embracing Grief

Grief, whether tied to loss, change, or unfulfilled desires, demands presence and care. The Black Madonna's connection to sorrow and resilience positions her as a figure of solace during periods of mourning. In her image, we see the acknowledgment of pain as a sacred part of the human experience—a necessary process that ultimately allows space for renewal.

In many depictions, the Black Madonna embodies the archetype of the mourning mother, her sorrow palpable yet dignified. This imagery resonates deeply with grieving people, as it offers permission to feel pain while simultaneously holding the promise of healing. The Black Madonna teaches that grief is not a weakness or failure but a testament to the depth of our love and humanity.

Practical Advice: Create rituals to honor your grief. Light a candle, speak aloud to the person or situation you are mourning, or engage in creative practices like painting, writing, or singing to express your emotions. These rituals can help transform grief into a source of connection and meaning.

Healing Trauma

Trauma often resides in the body and psyche, manifesting in patterns of fear, shame, or disconnection. With her maternal and nurturing qualities, the Black Madonna represents a safe space for exploring and healing trauma. Her dark complexion symbolizes the shadow work required to address these wounds, while her compassionate gaze invites us to treat ourselves with care and tenderness.

Trauma is complex and multi-faceted, often requiring both professional support and spiritual practices to heal. The Black Madonna reminds us that healing is a gradual, layered process. Her presence reassures us that even the most painful wounds can be transformed into sources of strength and wisdom when approached with patience and love.

In regions where the Black Madonna is venerated, she is often called upon by those who have experienced profound suffering, such as survivors of violence, displacement, or oppression. Her image symbolizes hope and resilience, reassuring that healing is possible despite adversity.

Practical Advice: If you are working through trauma, consider combining spiritual practices inspired by the Black

Madonna with professional therapeutic support. Practices like grounding, meditation, or prayer can help regulate emotions and provide a sense of safety, while therapy can offer tools to process and integrate your experiences.

Practical Steps To Heal With The Black Madonna

Acknowledge The Pain

1. The Black Madonna teaches that healing begins with acknowledgment. Denying or suppressing pain only allows it to grow in the shadows, while facing it directly allows transformation to begin.

Practical Advice: Set aside time for reflection, either through journaling, prayer, or silent meditation. Name the emotions or experiences you are grappling with, and allow yourself to feel them fully without judgment.

Lean Into Compassion

1. Her maternal nature reminds us that healing requires compassion—for ourselves and others. The Black Madonna invites us to release self-criticism and nurture our wounded parts with love and patience.

Practical Advice: Practice self-compassion by speaking kindly to yourself. Use affirmations such as, "I am worthy of healing" or "I am patient with myself as I grow."

Create Sacred Space For Healing

1. Healing requires a safe and sacred physical, emotional, or spiritual space. The Black Madonna's shrines, often

in caves or other secluded areas, symbolize this need for a protected environment where transformation can unfold.

Practical Advice: Dedicate a space in your home for reflection and healing. Add items that inspire peace, such as candles, images of the Black Madonna, or objects from nature. Use this space for meditation, prayer, or journaling when processing emotions.

Trust The Process

1. Healing is rarely linear. The Black Madonna's enduring image reminds us that transformation occurs beneath the surface, even in the darkest moments. Her presence reassures us that the journey, while challenging, leads to renewal.

Practical Advice: When healing feels slow or overwhelming, remember that progress unfolds in time. Consider keeping a journal to track small milestones or shifts in perspective, offering tangible evidence of your growth.

Real-World Examples

The Black Madonna is invoked in communities worldwide as a source of healing and strength. Survivors of personal and collective trauma often turn to her for guidance, comfort, and empowerment. For instance, in Haiti, syncretized figures like *Erzulie Dantor*, inspired by the Black Madonna, are called upon for protection and healing, especially by women who have endured hardship.

Similarly, Black Madonna shrines in Europe and Latin America are frequented by those seeking solace after loss, illness, or personal struggles. Pilgrimages to these sites are often deeply cathartic, allowing individuals to connect with her archetype and find renewed hope.

For spiritual seekers today, the Black Madonna's healing archetype invites them to approach fear, grief, and trauma not as enemies but as opportunities for profound transformation. By leaning into her symbolism and guidance, we learn to walk through the shadows with courage, emerging more substantial, whole, and connected to ourselves and the divine.

PRACTICES FOR SHADOW WORK INSPIRED BY THE BLACK MADONNA

Journaling, Meditations, And Rituals To Embrace The Shadow

The Black Madonna's symbolism provides a robust framework for shadow work, exploring and integrating the hidden or unacknowledged aspects of ourselves. Her connection to darkness and transformation invites us to approach this work with courage, compassion, and curiosity. By incorporating intentional practices such as journaling, meditation, and rituals, we can engage with the shadow self in meaningful and transformative ways.

Journaling: Exploring The Depths Of The Self

Journaling is a practical and accessible tool for uncovering and processing shadow aspects. Putting thoughts and emotions into words allows us to create a bridge between the unconscious and conscious mind, revealing patterns, beliefs, and feelings that may have remained hidden.

Shadow Journaling Prompts Inspired By The Black Madonna:

1. **Facing Fear:** Write about something that scares you. What is the source of this fear? How does it show up in your life, and what might it be trying to teach you?

2. **Embracing Vulnerability:** Reflect on a time when you felt vulnerable. How did you respond? What would it look like to approach vulnerability as a strength rather than a weakness?

3. **Hidden Desires:** Explore a part of yourself that you've repressed or denied. Why do you think you've hidden this part of yourself, and how might you begin to embrace it?

4. **The Darkness Within:** Describe what "darkness" means to you. Does it feel frightening, comforting, or something else entirely? How can you shift your perspective on the unknown?

Practical Advice: Dedicate a specific notebook or digital space for your shadow work. Write without judgment, allowing your thoughts and emotions to flow freely. Reread your entries periodically to notice patterns and growth over time.

Meditations: Connecting With The Energy Of The Black Madonna

Meditation offers a way to connect with the energy of the Black Madonna and create a safe space to engage with your shadow. Her presence, often depicted as nurturing yet firm, reminds us that we can approach this work with strength and gentleness.

Guided Meditation: Meeting The Black Madonna

1. Find a quiet space where you won't be disturbed. Sit comfortably, close your eyes, and take a few deep breaths to center yourself.

2. Visualize yourself entering a dark yet inviting cave, a sacred space that feels safe and nurturing. Imagine the flicker of candles illuminating the walls, casting soft, warm light.

3. You can see the Black Madonna seated on a throne at the center of the cave. Her dark, radiant presence exudes strength, compassion, and wisdom.

4. Approach her with a question or intention related to your shadow. For example, you might ask her to help you see a hidden part of yourself or guide you through a complex emotion.

5. Sit in her presence, listening and observing. Allow any thoughts, images, or sensations to arise without judgment.

6. When you feel ready, thank the Black Madonna for her guidance and slowly bring your awareness back to the present moment.

Practical Advice: Practice this meditation regularly, especially during emotional turmoil or introspection. You can modify it to include specific themes, such as addressing grief, fear, or self-doubt.

Rituals: Honoring The Shadow Through Sacred Action

Rituals offer a tangible way to engage with shadow work, transforming abstract emotions into physical acts of release and renewal. Inspired by the Black Madonna's symbolism, these rituals can help you embrace the darkness and invite healing.

Shadow Release Ritual:

1. **Prepare Your Space:** Choose a quiet, dimly lit area. Light a black candle to symbolize the shadow and a white candle to represent the light of awareness. Place a journal or piece of paper nearby.

2. **Set Your Intention:** Take a moment to reflect on what part of your shadow you wish to explore or release. Speak this intention aloud or write it down.

3. **Write and Burn:** On a piece of paper, write down any thoughts, feelings, or patterns you wish to confront and release. Once you've written everything, safely burn the paper, visualizing the smoke carrying these burdens away.

4. **Invite the Light:** Focus on the white candle, symbolizing the clarity and transformation from acknowledging your shadow. Spend a few moments in gratitude for the lessons your shadow has taught you.

Darkness Embrace Ritual:

1. **Create a Dark Space:** Turn off all lights or cover your windows to create complete darkness. Sit or lie down in

this space, allowing yourself to feel the stillness and mystery of the dark.

2. **Reflect and Listen:** Without distraction, reflect on what arises without light. Pay attention to any emotions, memories, or insights that emerge.

3. **Call on the Black Madonna:** Silently or aloud, invite the presence of the Black Madonna to guide and support you as you sit with the unknown.

4. **Close with Gratitude:** When ready, light a small candle or turn on a soft light, symbolizing the wisdom you've gained through the experience.

Practical Steps To Incorporate Shadow Work Into Daily Life

1. **Create a Consistent Practice:** Set aside regular time for shadow work, whether through journaling, meditation, or rituals. Consistency helps build trust in the process and allows deeper insights to emerge.

2. **Start Small:** Shadow work can feel overwhelming, so start with manageable practices, such as a five-minute reflection or a simple candle-lighting ritual.

3. **Seek Support:** If emotions or memories become too intense, consider working with a therapist or spiritual mentor. The Black Madonna's archetype reminds us that seeking help is an act of strength, not weakness.

4. **Celebrate Progress:** Acknowledge and celebrate the growth you experience, no matter how small. Shadow

work is an ongoing journey, and each step forward is a victory.

Real-World Applications

Shadow work practices inspired by the Black Madonna are used in retreats, spiritual circles, and therapeutic settings worldwide. Women's circles often incorporate journaling prompts, meditations, and rituals to help participants confront and integrate their shadow, fostering personal empowerment and collective healing.

In modern spirituality, these practices are particularly resonant for those exploring feminine empowerment. The Black Madonna's presence invites women to reclaim their complexity, embrace their depth, and honor the full spectrum of their experiences.

By engaging in these practices, we honor the Black Madonna's wisdom and bring light to the hidden parts of ourselves, transforming the shadow into a source of strength, self-awareness, and healing.

7: BLACK MADONNA AND FEMININE EMPOWERMENT

"She is both the mother and the warrior, holding the mysteries of the universe within her gaze, inviting us to step into our own power."

RECLAIMING THE DIVINE FEMININE

THE FEMININE IN BALANCE WITH THE MASCULINE

How The Black Madonna Teaches Integration Of Opposites

With her compelling presence and profound symbolism, the Black Madonna embodies the wisdom of balance—notably the harmony between the feminine and masculine energies that exist within all of us. Unlike traditional depictions of the Virgin Mary, who often embodies pure maternal nurturing, the Black Madonna is fierce yet compassionate, mysterious yet illuminating. She represents an integrated divine feminine that unionizes with the sacred masculine, teaching us that balance between these forces is the key to personal and collective empowerment.

Her archetype reminds us that neither the feminine nor the

masculine exists in isolation; they are complementary energies that, when united, create wholeness. The Black Madonna invites us to embrace this integration within ourselves and our relationships, challenging societal narratives that often pit these energies against or elevate one over the other.

The Feminine As Intuition And Creation

In spiritual traditions, feminine energy is often associated with intuition, receptivity, creation, and nurturing. These attributes align with the mysteries of the Black Madonna, who is deeply connected to the earth, the cycles of nature, and the unseen forces of the universe. Her dark complexion symbolizes the fertile soil of creation and the void from which all life emerges, reminding us that the feminine is powerful and essential.

The Black Madonna's fierce maternal energy also speaks to the protective and creative aspects of the feminine. She is not a passive nurturer but an active force of transformation. Like the earth, she sustains life while holding the power to dismantle and recreate. In this way, she encourages us to embrace our creative and intuitive capacities without fear, trusting the process of growth and renewal.

The Masculine As Action And Structure

While the feminine embodies receptivity and creation, the masculine energy complements it through action, structure, and purpose. In many spiritual traditions, the masculine is represented by focus, logic, and the drive to bring ideas into form. While deeply connected to feminine energy, the Black Madonna reflects this masculine aspect through her strength and unwavering presence. She is a protector, a guardian of sacred spaces, and a force that takes action when needed.

As a bridge between the feminine and masculine, the Black Madonna teaches us that these energies are not opposites to be reconciled but partners to be harmonized. Just as the feminine gives birth to ideas, the masculine provides the structure to manifest them. Together, they create a dynamic balance that is essential for wholeness.

Integration Of Opposites: Lessons From The Black Madonna

The Black Madonna's ability to embody feminine and masculine energies teaches us the importance of integrating opposites within ourselves. Many of us lean too heavily into one energy while neglecting the other, creating imbalance. For instance, focusing solely on masculine traits like productivity and logic can lead to burnout, while over-identifying with feminine characteristics like intuition and creativity may result in a lack of direction.

The Black Madonna's presence calls us to bring these energies into harmony. Her dark, mysterious energy invites us to honor the feminine qualities of introspection and creation, while her strength and protective nature remind us of the importance of action and structure. This balance is not about suppressing one energy in favor of the other but about allowing both to flow to support our growth and empowerment.

Practical Lessons For Integration:

Honor The Feminine And Masculine Within

1. Recognize that you carry both energies within you, regardless of gender. Embrace the strengths of each energy and understand that they work best in partnership.

Practical Advice: Reflect on which energy you lean more heavily daily. If you notice an imbalance, intentionally cultivate the opposite energy. For example, if you focus primarily on productivity (masculine), schedule time for creative or reflective activities (feminine). Another example could be to balance your work tasks with self-care activities, such as taking a walk in nature or practicing mindfulness.

Balance Action With Rest

1. The Black Madonna teaches that rest is as vital as action. The feminine energy of rest allows you to recharge and connect with your intuition, while the masculine energy of action moves you toward your goals.

Practical Advice: Create a daily rhythm that honors both energies. For instance, begin your day with a feminine practice like meditation or journaling, and then shift into focused action for your tasks.

Integrate Intuition And Logic

1. The Black Madonna's wisdom lies in blending the intuitive with the logical. She reminds us that decisions

made with the heart and the mind are often the most aligned.

Practical Advice: When deciding, balance your intuitive insights with sensible considerations. Ask yourself, "What feels right?" and "What makes sense?" Trust that both perspectives hold value.

Real-World Applications

The Black Madonna's teachings on integrating feminine and masculine energies are especially relevant in today's world, where imbalance often dominates. In patriarchal societies, masculine traits like dominance and competition are often elevated, suppressing feminine qualities such as empathy and collaboration. Conversely, in environments where passivity prevails, the assertive action of the masculine is sometimes underutilized.

In workplaces, for example, leaders who embody both feminine and masculine energies—compassionate yet decisive, intuitive yet strategic—tend to foster more balanced and effective teams. The Black Madonna's archetype is a model for this kind of integrated leadership, encouraging both men and women to lead with heart and purpose.

Integrating these energies can lead to greater personal empowerment for individuals. By embracing the feminine aspects of creativity and introspection alongside the masculine qualities of structure and action, we can approach life's challenges with a sense of wholeness and adaptability.

Balancing feminine and masculine energies fosters harmony and mutual respect in relationships. The Black Madonna's presence reminds us that true partnership arises when both energies are honored and allowed to coexist within ourselves or others.

Practical advice: To explore these dynamics, reflect on how feminine and masculine energies appear in your relationships. Can you express both vulnerability (feminine) and boundaries (masculine)? Practice cultivating both energies to create a more profound balance and connection.

The Black Madonna teaches that integration is not about perfection but about embracing the dynamic interplay of opposites. Through her example, we learn that the harmony of the feminine and masculine within ourselves is possible and essential for living an empowered and authentic life.

EMPOWERMENT THROUGH HER STORIES

Lessons Of Resilience, Creativity, And Nurturing Strength From The Black Madonna

The Black Madonna's stories, steeped in legend and devotion, reveal her as a figure of profound empowerment. Across cultures and centuries, she has been celebrated as a source of divine protection and a symbol of resilience, creativity, and nurturing strength. Her narratives carry universal lessons for those seeking to reclaim their power, reminding us that adversity can be transformed into growth and that strength and compassion are not opposites but allies.

The Black Madonna inspires us to navigate life's challenges with grace and creativity, embodying both the fierce protector and the nurturing guide. Through her stories, she demonstrates that empowerment is not about domination but about embracing one's wholeness—finding strength in vulnerability, power in compassion, and creativity in chaos.

Resilience In Adversity

Throughout her legends, the Black Madonna is often depicted as a protector and healer in times of crisis. Whether safeguarding communities from invaders, as in the story of Our Lady of Częstochowa in Poland or providing miraculous interventions during natural disasters, her presence symbolizes resilience in the face of adversity. Her dark skin, often seen as a reflection of the earth itself, reminds us of the cycles of destruction and renewal that define nature and human experience.

In Haiti, for instance, the syncretized Black Madonna, *Erzulie Dantor*, is revered as a fierce protector of women, children, and the oppressed. Her story of survival and strength resonates deeply with those who have endured hardship, offering a reminder that resilience is born from both struggle and love.

Lesson: Resilience is not the absence of hardship but the ability to rise, adapt, and find meaning in the face of challenges. The Black Madonna teaches us that we can draw strength from our experiences, even the painful ones, and use them as a foundation for growth.

Practical Advice: Reflect on a time when you overcame adversity. What inner resources helped you navigate that experience? How might you draw on those strengths to face current challenges? Journaling about these reflections can help you reconnect with your resilience.

Creativity As A Path To Empowerment

The Black Madonna's association with the earth and fertility underscores her connection to creativity—not just in the literal sense of giving life but also in the broader sense of birthing new ideas, perspectives, and possibilities. Her stories often take place in sacred spaces like caves, mountains, and forests, symbolizing the womb of creation.

In Spain, *La Moreneta* of Montserrat is said to have been discovered in a cave by shepherds. This setting, rich with symbolism, reminds us that creativity often arises from places of mystery and introspection. The Black Madonna teaches that even in the darkest moments, we can create something meaningful, whether a solution to a problem, a work of art, or a new chapter in our lives.

Lesson: Creativity is a tool for empowerment. It allows us to reimagine our circumstances and transform limitations into opportunities. By embracing our creative potential, we can find new ways to navigate life's challenges and express our authentic selves.

Practical Advice: Cultivate creativity by engaging in practices that inspire you, such as painting, writing, cooking, or gardening. When facing a problem, approach it with curiosity and ask, "What new solution can I create from this situation?"

Nurturing Strength

The Black Madonna's nurturing energy is often depicted in her role as a mother. Yet, her nurturing is not passive or submissive but active, protective, and transformative. She embodies the archetype of the "warrior mother," who nurtures with fierce love while defending what she holds sacred.

In Brazil, Our Lady of Aparecida is seen as a mother to all, particularly the poor and marginalized. Her story of miraculous discovery in the Paraíba River speaks to her ability to uplift those who feel unseen or forgotten. Her nurturing strength reminds us that care and compassion are not signs of weakness but powerful forces for change.

Lesson: Nurturing strength lies in the ability to care deeply for others and ourselves while remaining grounded in our power. The Black Madonna shows us that love, far from being a vulnerability, is one of our most significant sources of strength.

Practical Advice: Practice self-nurturing by prioritizing rest, nourishment, and activities that bring you joy. Extend your nurturing strength outward by supporting others in meaningful ways, whether through acts of kindness, listening, or offering encouragement.

Practical Steps For Empowerment Through Her Stories

Draw On Her Resilience

1. Use the Black Madonna's stories as inspiration when facing challenges. Meditate on her image or keep a representation of her in your space to remind you of

the strength and resilience you carry within.

Foster Creativity in Times of Change

1. When life feels uncertain or overwhelming, channel your energy into creative practices. The Black Madonna's connection to the cycles of nature can serve as a reminder that creativity often arises from periods of transition and renewal.

Balance, Strength, and Compassion

1. Reflect on how the Black Madonna balances fierce strength with nurturing love. Consider how you integrate these qualities into your life, whether in your relationships, work, or personal growth.

Real-World Applications

The Black Madonna's resilience, creativity, and nurturing strength lessons resonate deeply with those seeking feminine empowerment in modern times. In personal development workshops, her stories often inspire participants to reclaim their power and embrace their authenticity. Artists, writers, and healers frequently draw on her archetype to explore themes of transformation, motherhood, and the divine feminine.

Her influence can also be seen in social justice and equality movements. The Black Madonna's legacy as a protector of the oppressed inspires activists to approach their work passionately and compassionately, fostering change while remaining connected to their humanity.

For spiritual seekers, her stories remind them that

empowerment is not about erasing challenges but embracing them as growth opportunities. Embodying her resilience, creativity, and nurturing strength, we can navigate life's complexities with grace, courage, and purpose.

ACTIVATING FEMININE POWER IN A MODERN WORLD

Practical Steps To Connect With The Black Madonna's Energy

The Black Madonna represents a deep wellspring of feminine power that is both timeless and profoundly relevant to the modern world. Her energy invites us to embrace the complexities of life—strength and vulnerability, light and shadow, action and reflection—while challenging us to embody our authentic selves. Activating feminine power through her archetype isn't about adopting rigid practices or ideals but about tuning into the dynamic and creative force she symbolizes, adapting her lessons to our unique journeys.

By consciously connecting with the Black Madonna's energy, we can cultivate inner strength, creativity, and a sense of purpose in the face of life's demands. Through practical steps that integrate her wisdom into daily life, she becomes a guide for navigating modern challenges with grace, resilience, and empowerment.

1. Create A Sacred Space For Reflection

The Black Madonna is often venerated in sacred spaces— mountains, caves, and shrines that evoke mystery and introspection. Creating your own sacred space at home can help you connect with her energy and honor the divine feminine within.

Practical advice: Dedicate a small area in your home for spiritual reflection. Include symbols that resonate with the Black Madonna, such as candles, images, flowers, or natural objects like stones or branches. Use this space for meditation, prayer, journaling, or sitting still.

2. Connect With The Cycles Of Nature

The Black Madonna's connection to the earth reminds us of the importance of aligning with natural rhythms. In a fast-paced world that often demands constant productivity, reconnecting with nature's cycles can restore balance and foster a sense of groundedness.

Practical Advice: Spend time outdoors to observe and honor nature's rhythms. Whether walking barefoot on the earth, planting a garden, or simply sitting under a tree, these practices can help you attune to the energy of the Black Madonna. Reflect on how growth, decay, and renewal cycles mirror your own experiences.

3. Embrace Intuition And Inner Knowing

The Black Madonna symbolizes the feminine quality of intuition—a deep inner wisdom that often speaks in subtle ways. Modern life's emphasis on logic and external validation can make it challenging to trust this inner voice. Cultivating intuition is an essential step in activating feminine power.

Practical Advice: Practice tuning into your intuition by starting small. When faced with a decision, pause and notice what your body and emotions tell you. Keep a journal to track intuitive insights and how they play out over time. Meditation and mindfulness practices can also help quiet the mind, making it easier to hear your inner voice.

4. Honor The Power Of Vulnerability

The Black Madonna's strength is rooted in her ability to hold space for grief, fear, and other vulnerable emotions. She reminds us that vulnerability is not a weakness but a source of power and connection. Embracing this truth can be transformative, allowing us to show up authentically in our relationships and the world.

Practical Advice: Start by acknowledging your emotions without judgment. If you're comfortable, share your vulnerabilities with someone you trust, whether through a heartfelt conversation or creative expression. Cultivate self-compassion as you navigate this process, using affirmations such as, "It's safe for me to be seen as I am."

5. Engage In Rituals Of Empowerment

Rituals are a powerful way to embody the energy of the Black Madonna and activate feminine power. They provide structure and intention, bridging the spiritual and the practical.

Practical Advice:

- **Morning Empowerment Ritual:** Begin your day by lighting a candle and speaking an affirmation inspired by the Black Madonna, such as, "I embrace my strength, my shadow, and my light."

- **Complete Moon Ritual:** Use the full moon's energy to release what no longer serves you and set intentions for growth. Write down limiting beliefs or fears and burn the paper as an act of letting go, calling on the Black Madonna for guidance.

- **Creative Ritual:** Engage in a creative activity, such as painting, writing, or dancing, as an offering to the Black Madonna. Allow this practice to celebrate your feminine energy and unique self-expression.

6. Support Community And Collaboration

The Black Madonna is a unifying figure, often celebrated as a protector of the marginalized and a force for social justice. Activating feminine power involves stepping beyond individual empowerment to support community and collaboration, embodying the nurturing and inclusive qualities she represents.

Practical Advice: Look for ways to uplift others in your community. This could be through volunteering, joining a women's circle, mentoring someone, or advocating for social justice causes. Collaboration and mutual support amplify the collective's power, reflecting the Black Madonna's interconnected energy.

7. Balance Rest And Action

Feminine power requires honoring both stillness and movement. The Black Madonna teaches that rest is not idleness but an essential part of renewal. Balancing periods of action with moments of rest ensures sustainability and prevents burnout, allowing you to show up fully in all areas of life.

Practical Advice: Schedule regular downtime for reflection, relaxation, and self-care. Use these moments to reconnect with your inner self and recharge. Then, when it's time to take action, move with intention and focus, trusting in your renewed energy.

Real-World Applications

Women and men worldwide draw on the Black Madonna's energy to navigate modern life's complexities. From personal development workshops to spiritual retreats, her archetype is used as a model for integrating strength and compassion, intuition and logic, action and rest. Activating feminine power through her wisdom has inspired leaders, healers, and activists to embrace authenticity, creativity, and collaboration in their work and relationships.

In today's fast-paced world, the Black Madonna reminds us that true empowerment is rooted in balance. By connecting with her energy, we can cultivate resilience, nurture our inner world, and contribute to society's collective healing and transformation.

Practical Advice: Begin by incorporating one practice that resonates with you—creating a sacred space, honoring nature, or engaging in an empowerment ritual. Let the Black Madonna's energy guide you as you step into your power, embracing the challenges and beauty of the modern world with grace and confidence.

8: RITUALS AND SACRED PRACTICES FOR CONNECTING WITH THE BLACK MADONNA

"To stand before the Black Madonna is to touch the pulse of humanity's shared struggles, triumphs, and the eternal bond of mother and child."

WAYS TO HONOR HER ENERGY

CREATING A BLACK MADONNA ALTAR

How To Build A Sacred Space To Connect With Her

An altar dedicated to the Black Madonna is more than a physical space; it is a sanctuary where her energy can be invoked, honored, and felt. Building a Black Madonna altar is a deeply personal act of devotion and intention, reflecting your connection to her as a symbol of the divine feminine transformation and empowerment. This sacred space becomes a focal point for rituals, meditation, and prayer, bridging your everyday life and the mysteries she represents.

By carefully selecting items that resonate with the Black Madonna's energy and symbolism, you can create a robust environment to honor her presence, foster reflection, and deepen your spiritual journey.

Step-By-Step Guide To Creating A Black Madonna Altar

Choose a Dedicated Space

1. The location of your altar should feel sacred and intentional. This could be a corner of a room, a small table, or even a windowsill. Consider a space where you can sit quietly and connect without distraction.

Practical Advice: Place your altar near natural light or in a peaceful, grounding location. For added significance, choose a place associated with personal transformation or healing.

Select A Representation Of The Black Madonna

1. The centerpiece of your altar should be an image or statue of the Black Madonna that resonates with you. This could be a traditional depiction from a specific culture, such as Our Lady of Częstochowa or Montserrat, or a modern interpretation reflecting her energy.

Practical Advice: If you cannot find an image or statue, consider creating your own through art or printing an image that speaks to you. Trust your intuition to guide your choice.

Incorporate Symbols Of Her Energy

1. The Black Madonna is often associated with earth, shadow, and mystery elements. Including symbols that reflect these aspects can help anchor her energy in your altar space.

    - **Earth elements:** Stones, crystals (such as black

- obsidian, onyx, or smoky quartz), or soil to honor her connection to the earth.

- **Candles:** A black candle represents shadow and mystery, and a white candle symbolizes illumination and transformation.

- **Flowers:** Dark or richly colored blooms, such as roses or lilies, reflect her nurturing and regenerative qualities.

- **Sacred items:** Feathers, shells, or personal objects that carry meaning for you.

Add Layers Of Meaning

Personalize your altar with items that reflect your unique connection to the Black Madonna. This could include objects from nature, such as a seashell from a meaningful beach, spiritual tools like a favorite crystal, or mementos tied to your journey, like a photo of a loved one. These personal touches can enhance your connection to the altar and the Black Madonna. **Practical advice:** Consider including a journal or small notebook to record reflections, prayers, or insights that arise during your time at the altar.

Infuse The Space With Scent And Sound

1. Engaging the senses can enhance your experience at the altar and create a deeper connection with the Black Madonna's energy.

Practical Advice: Burn incense, sage, or palo santo to cleanse the space and invoke her presence. Consider using essential oils, such as frankincense, myrrh, or sandalwood, often associated with sacred rituals. You might also play soft music, chant, or sit silently to allow her energy to flow.

Rituals To Activate And Use Your Altar

Once your Black Madonna altar is complete, it becomes a space for ongoing connection and devotion. Here are a few rituals you can perform at your altar:

Morning Or Evening Prayer:

1. Begin or end your day by lighting a candle and offering a prayer or affirmation to the Black Madonna. Speak from your heart, expressing gratitude or asking for guidance.

Shadow Work Meditation:

1. Sit at your altar and meditate on an aspect of your shadow self you wish to explore. Visualize the Black Madonna's presence, offering her wisdom and support as you reflect.

Creative Ritual:

1. Use your altar to engage in creative activities like journaling, painting, or writing. Dedicate your creative expression to the Black Madonna, allowing her energy to inspire and guide you.

Seasonal Offerings:

1. Honor nature's cycles by changing the items on your altar to reflect the seasons. For example, in spring, you might include fresh flowers and symbols of renewal,

while in winter, you might add evergreen branches and candles.

Release and Renewal Ceremony:

1. Write down fears, doubts, or limiting beliefs on paper. Burn the paper in a fire-safe bowl or container at your altar, visualizing the Black Madonna helping you release these burdens. Follow this with gratitude for the clarity and space you've created.

Practical Tips For Maintaining Your Altar

- **Regularly Cleanse the Space:** Use smoke, sound, or intention to cleanse your altar and refresh its energy. This helps maintain its sacredness and strengthens the connection to the Black Madonna.

- **Rotate Items as Needed:** Update the altar to reflect changes in your spiritual journey or life circumstances. This keeps the space dynamic and meaningful.

- **Use the Altar Daily:** Frequent use of your altar, whether through meditation, prayer, or simple reflection, deepens your relationship with the Black Madonna and strengthens your spiritual practice.

Real-World Applications

Creating a Black Madonna altar is a deeply personal and transformative act. Across the world, individuals and communities use altars to honor the divine feminine, connect with their inner wisdom, and anchor themselves in the sacred. Whether in homes, retreat spaces, or places of worship, these altars become focal points for empowerment, healing, and spiritual exploration.

For modern spiritual seekers, a Black Madonna altar grounds feminine empowerment in daily life. It reminds us of her qualities—resilience, nurturing strength, and creative power—and encourages us to embody those qualities as we navigate the complexities of the modern world.

By creating and using your altar with intention, you open a channel for the Black Madonna's energy to flow into your life, supporting your journey of self-discovery, empowerment, and transformation.

RITUALS FOR HEALING AND TRANSFORMATION

Steps For Rituals Inspired By Her Global Traditions

The Black Madonna has long been associated with healing and transformation, and the rituals connected to her are as diverse as the cultures that honor her. From the shrines of Europe to the syncretic traditions of the Americas, her presence is invoked to restore balance, heal emotional wounds, and facilitate profound spiritual renewal. These rituals often draw upon her dual nature as both a nurturer and a powerful protector, reflecting her ability to hold space for shadow and light, destruction and rebirth. Her influence can be seen in the Black Madonna of Częstochowa in Poland, the Montserrat Virgin in Spain, and in the syncretic traditions of the Americas, where she is often associated with the Orishas of the Yoruba religion.

Incorporating rituals inspired by the global traditions of the Black Madonna into your spiritual practice allows you to tap into her transformative energy. These sacred acts, steeped in devotion and symbolism, create an opportunity for connection, introspection, and renewal.

1. A Ritual Of Emotional Healing

The Black Madonna is often called upon to comfort those experiencing grief, fear, or emotional pain. This ritual draws on her nurturing and maternal energy to create space for emotional release and self-compassion.

Steps For Emotional Healing Ritual

1. **Preparation:**

   - Choose a quiet space where you feel safe and comfortable.

   - Place a dark-colored candle (black or deep blue) on your altar or in front of you, representing the depth of the emotions you wish to explore.

   - Include objects that comfort you, such as a soft scarf, a favorite flower, or an image of the Black Madonna.

2. **Set Your Intention:**

Sit still and reflect on what emotions or wounds you are ready to acknowledge and begin healing. Speak your intention aloud, such as:

   - *"Black Madonna, guide me as I honor and release my pain. Help me find healing and strength within."*

1. **Light the Candle:**

   - As you light the candle, visualize the flame as a symbol of her presence. Imagine her nurturing energy surrounding you, creating a protective and compassionate space.

2. **Emotional Release:**

   - Write down your feelings, memories, or fears on paper. Allow yourself to express yourself freely and without judgment. If tears or emotions arise, let them flow. The Black Madonna holds space for all that you carry.

3. **Release and Transform:**

   - Safely burn the paper in a fireproof bowl or container. As the smoke rises, imagine the Black Madonna transforming your pain into light and renewal.

4. **Close with Gratitude:**

   - Thank the Black Madonna for her guidance. Extinguish the candle, knowing her energy remains with you.

Frequency: Use this ritual to process and release heavy emotions.

2. A Ritual Of Shadow Work And Transformation

Inspired by her connection to the shadow self, this ritual helps you confront and integrate hidden aspects of your personality. Drawing on her symbolic association with the earth and the womb of creation, this practice facilitates deep self-reflection and transformation.

Steps For Shadow Work Ritual

1. **Prepare the Space:**

   - Conduct this ritual at night or in a dimly lit room to evoke the sacred mystery of the Black Madonna.

   - Place a black stone (obsidian, onyx, or smoky quartz) and a white candle on your altar to symbolize the balance of shadow and light.

2. **Ground Yourself:**

   - Begin with deep breaths or a grounding exercise. Visualize yourself rooted in the earth, drawing stability and strength from its depths.

3. **Invoke the Black Madonna:**

Say a prayer or affirmation to invite her guidance:

   - *"Black Madonna, help me see what lies hidden within. Illuminate my shadow and show me the path to wholeness."*

1. **Reflect on Your Shadow:**

   - Use a journal to explore parts of yourself that feel suppressed, ignored, or misunderstood. Ask questions such as:

     - What triggers me, and why?

     - What do I avoid or fear in myself?

     - How can I honor this part of me instead of rejecting it?

2. **Meditate on Transformation:**

- Hold the black stone in your hand and visualize it absorbing your fears, doubts, or suppressed emotions. Then, focus on the white candle, imagining its light filling the space within you that was once hidden in darkness.

3. **Close with a Ritual Offering:**

   - Offer flowers, incense, or a small token of gratitude to the Black Madonna, symbolizing your commitment to self-awareness and growth.

Frequency: Perform this ritual during significant life transitions or when you feel ready to explore your inner depths.

3. A Ritual For Collective Healing And Empowerment

The Black Madonna is revered as a protector of communities, particularly the marginalized and oppressed. This ritual channels her energy to promote collective healing and empowerment, making it ideal for group settings or acts of social advocacy.

Steps for Collective Healing Ritual

1. **Gather the Group:**

   - Bring together people with a shared intention for healing, whether for a specific cause, community, or the world.

   - Create a central altar featuring an image of the Black Madonna, candles, and symbolic items representing the collective intention (e.g., a globe, a heart-shaped object, or protest signs).

2. **Set the Collective Intention:**

Invite each participant to share their intention or prayer for healing and empowerment. For example:

- *"We call on the Black Madonna to guide us in creating justice, healing wounds, and nurturing hope for all."*

1. **Light the Candles:**

   - Light multiple candles to symbolize the group's shared energy and connection. As the candles burn, visualize the Black Madonna's protective and empowering presence embracing the community or cause.

2. **Collective Offering:**

   - Invite participants to offer a symbolic action, such as placing flowers, written prayers, or stones on the altar. This act represents unity and shared purpose.

3. **Chant or Meditate Together:**

   - Chant a mantra or meditate in silence to amplify the group's collective energy. Suggested mantra: *"Black Madonna, guardian of the oppressed, guide us in love, strength, and action."*

4. **Closing Gratitude:**

   - Thank the Black Madonna for her guidance and commitment to carrying her energy into the world through actions of love and justice.

Frequency: Perform this ritual during times of collective need, such as after a tragedy, during activism efforts, or to celebrate community resilience.

Real-World Inspirations

Across the world, rituals dedicated to the Black Madonna inspire healing and transformation on both personal and collective levels. Pilgrimages to her shrines, such as Montserrat in Spain or Jasna Góra in Poland, often include acts of devotion similar to these rituals—prayers for healing, offerings of gratitude, and symbolic acts of surrender and renewal.

For modern spiritual seekers, these rituals provide a way to honor their traditions while addressing contemporary challenges. They remind us that healing and empowerment are sacred processes deeply connected to the wisdom of the divine feminine.

Engaging in rituals inspired by the Black Madonna creates opportunities to release burdens, reclaim your strength, and align with her transformative energy. Through her stories, symbols, and sacred practices, she remains a timeless guide for navigating the complexities of healing and transformation in today's world.

CHANTS, PRAYERS, AND MEDITATIONS

Specific Practices To Align With Her Sacred Energy

Chants, prayers, and meditations dedicated to the Black Madonna are profoundly effective ways to align with her transformative energy. Across cultures, these practices have invoked her presence, expressed devotion, and sought guidance in times of uncertainty, grief, or transition. By incorporating these sacred practices into your spiritual routine, you create a direct channel to connect with her empowering and nurturing essence, inviting her wisdom and protection into your life.

These practices, rooted in global traditions, can be adapted to your intentions, whether you seek healing, resilience, clarity, or deeper self-awareness.

1. Chants To Invoke Her Energy

Chanting is a powerful way to invoke the Black Madonna's energy. Repeating sacred phrases or sounds creates a meditative state, allowing you to attune to her frequency and open your heart to her presence.

Chant For Resilience And Strength

"O Mater Nigra, dona nobis fortitudinem."

(Translation: "O Black Mother, grant us strength.")

- **Purpose:** This chant draws on the Black Madonna's strength and resilience, especially during struggle or self-doubt.

- **How to Practice:** Sit quietly, close your eyes, and chant the phrase slowly and rhythmically. Visualize the Black Madonna's protective energy surrounding you like a warm, dark cloak, grounding and empowering you.

Chant for Healing and Renewal

"Mater Dolorosa, salve vulnera nostra."

(Translation: "Mother of Sorrows, heal our wounds.")

- **Purpose:** This chant is ideal for emotional or physical healing, as it invokes the compassionate and nurturing aspect of the Black Madonna.

- **How to Practice:** Light a candle and chant this phrase softly, focusing on the area of your life or body that needs healing. Imagine her hands gently offering solace and renewal.

Chant For Shadow Work

"Ad tenebras lucem duc."

(Translation: "Bring light to the shadows.")

- **Purpose:** Use this chant when engaging in introspection or shadow work. It calls on the Black Madonna to illuminate the hidden aspects of yourself that need integration.

- **How to Practice:** Chant this phrase during meditation or while journaling. Visualize the Black Madonna's light, which will reveal what lies in your inner darkness and offer clarity and understanding.

-

2. Prayers To Deepen Connection

Prayers to the Black Madonna are personal and heartfelt, often addressing her as a mother, protector, and guide. Below are sample prayers you can use or adapt to suit your needs.

Prayer for Protection

"O Black Madonna, guardian of the forgotten and shield for the vulnerable, surround me with your strength. Protect me

from harm, guide me through darkness, and help me stand firm in adversity. With your fierce love, keep me safe and grounded, now and always. Amen."

- **When to Use:** During times of uncertainty, fear, or when you feel the need for her protective energy.

Prayer for Inner Peace

"Mother of Mystery, calm the storms within me. Help me embrace the unknown with trust and courage. Lead me to the still waters of your wisdom, where I may find peace in your loving presence. Teach me to surrender, knowing that everything is in your care. Amen."

- **When to Use:** When seeking clarity, calm, or guidance in emotional or mental turmoil.

Prayer for Feminine Empowerment

"O Sacred Mother, you who hold the strength of the earth and the wisdom of the stars awaken the power within me. Teach me to honor my intuition, trust my voice, and walk with courage and compassion. May your light guide me as I step fully into my power. Amen."

- **When to Use:** To reconnect with your inner strength, confidence, and authentic self.

3. Meditations to Align with Her Energy

Meditation creates a quiet space where you can connect deeply with the Black Madonna's energy, allowing her presence to inspire healing, insight, and transformation.

Meditation For Grounding And Stability

1. **Preparation:** Sit comfortably on the floor or in a chair with your feet touching the ground. Place a small black stone (obsidian or hematite) in your hands.

2. **Visualize:** Close your eyes and imagine roots growing from your body into the earth, anchoring you deeply. See the Black Madonna standing beside you, her hands resting gently on your shoulders. Feel her grounding energy stabilizing you.

3. **Affirm:** Silently or aloud, repeat the affirmation: *"I am grounded, safe, and held by the earth's embrace."*

4. **Close:** Spend a few moments in gratitude before opening your eyes.

Meditation For Embracing The Shadow

1. **Preparation:** Light a black candle and sit in a dimly lit or dark room. Place an image of the Black Madonna before you.

2. **Visualize:** Imagine the Black Madonna emerging from the darkness, holding a glowing orb of light. Her light gently illuminates your inner shadows as she approaches—areas of fear, shame, or pain.

3. **Reflect:** Allow whatever arises to come into awareness without judgment. Imagine the Black Madonna offering her wisdom and compassion as you explore these hidden parts of yourself.

4. **Release:** Visualize her light, dissolving and

transforming your fears into strength and understanding.

Meditation For Feminine Empowerment

1. **Preparation:** Surround yourself with symbols of the Black Madonna, such as flowers, candles, or sacred objects.

2. **Visualize:** Close your eyes and picture the Black Madonna standing in a radiant circle of light. She extends her hands to you, inviting you into the circle.

3. **Affirm:** As you enter the circle, feel her energy filling you with courage, creativity, and confidence. Repeat silently or aloud: *"I am whole, I am powerful, I am divine."*

4. **Close:** Sit quietly in her presence, absorbing her energy. When ready, open your eyes and carry her empowerment into your day.

Practical Tips For Incorporating Chants, Prayers, And Meditations

- **Daily Practice:** Dedicate a few minutes each day to one of these practices to maintain a consistent connection with the Black Madonna's energy.

- **Combine Practices:** Begin with a chant to invoke her energy, meditate, and close with a prayer to create a well-rounded spiritual session.

- **Adapt for Group Settings:** Chants and prayers can be

- used in women's circles, retreats, or other group gatherings to amplify her energy and foster collective empowerment.

Real-World Applications

Chants, prayers, and meditations inspired by the Black Madonna are used by spiritual practitioners worldwide to cultivate resilience, healing, and empowerment. From private devotions at home to communal gatherings at her shrines, these practices embody her timeless wisdom and transformative power.

For those navigating the complexities of modern life, these sacred practices offer a moment of pause, reflection, and connection to the divine feminine. Through her energy, the Black Madonna teaches us to embrace the depth of our inner world, transform challenges into opportunities, and walk our path with strength, compassion, and authenticity.

9: BLACK MADONNA AND THE CYCLE OF LIFE

"She wears the skin of the earth, embodying the diversity of all people and the infinite faces of the divine feminine."

BIRTH, DEATH, AND REBIRTH IN HER SYMBOLISM

HOW THE BLACK MADONNA REPRESENTS LIFE'S TRANSITIONS

Navigating Personal Growth Through Her Archetype

The Black Madonna embodies the life cycle—birth, death, and rebirth—offering wisdom for navigating the transitions that define our existence. As an archetype, she represents the fullness of life's journey, holding space for creation, loss, and renewal. Her dark visage and maternal presence invite us to embrace these cycles with trust and courage, reminding us that every ending carries the seed of a new beginning.

By reflecting on her symbolism, we can find guidance and empowerment during personal growth and transformation. Whether navigating loss, pursuing change, or seeking renewal, the Black Madonna serves as a sacred mirror for our experiences, teaching us to honor life's transitions as holy opportunities for growth.

The Black Madonna As A Symbol Of Birth

The Black Madonna is deeply connected to the mysteries of creation, symbolized by her association with the earth and the womb. Her dark skin reflects the fertile soil where seeds are planted, gestating in darkness before bursting into life. This symbolism makes her a powerful guide for those embarking on new beginnings, whether through creative projects, relationships, or personal transformations.

As a maternal figure, the Black Madonna's nurturing presence offers support and reassurance during the vulnerable stages of birth—both literal and metaphorical. She teaches us that all beginnings require preparation, patience, and trust in the unseen forces behind the scenes.

Practical Advice: When starting something new, create a ritual to honor the birth of your intentions. Light a candle at your altar and speak your goals aloud, asking the Black Madonna to bless and nurture your endeavors. Keep a journal to track the "seeds" you are planting and their progress.

The Black Madonna As A Guide Through Death

In the symbolic sense, death represents endings, loss, and the shedding of what no longer serves us. The Black Madonna's presence in the shadow and her connection to sorrow and grief make her a compassionate guide during these challenging transitions. She encourages us to face endings with courage, knowing they are essential to life's rhythm.

Her archetype reminds us that death is not something to be feared but a necessary transformation phase. Just as the earth rests in winter, allowing for renewal in spring, endings create the space needed for new growth. The Black Madonna's ability to hold both sorrow and hope inspires us to honor the pain of loss while remaining open to the following possibilities.

Practical Advice: When navigating an ending, create a ceremony to release what you are letting go of. Write down your thoughts, emotions, or attachments on paper and burn them safely, visualizing the Black Madonna guiding you through the transition. Allow yourself to grieve, knowing this process creates fertile ground for renewal.

The Black Madonna As A Symbol Of Rebirth

Rebirth is the culmination of life's cycles, symbolizing renewal, transformation, and the emergence of new life. The Black Madonna, often depicted with a child or surrounded by symbols of growth, embodies the promise of rebirth that follows periods of darkness. She reminds us that every challenge and loss carries the potential for profound renewal, urging us to trust in the transformation process.

Her archetype teaches us that rebirth is not about returning to who we were but about becoming something new. Through the trials of death and the gestation of the unknown, we are reshaped into more substantial, wiser, and authentic versions of ourselves. The Black Madonna's resilience and unwavering presence encourage us to embrace these moments of renewal with hope and gratitude.

Practical Advice: To honor a personal rebirth, create a ritual celebrating your transformation. Spend time reflecting on the growth you have experienced, and write affirmations or intentions for the new chapter of your life. Decorate your altar with symbols of renewal, such as flowers, seeds, or a white candle, and offer gratitude to the Black Madonna for her guidance.

Using The Black Madonna's Archetype For Personal Growth

The Black Madonna's symbolism provides a roadmap for navigating the cycles of life with intention and grace. By working with her archetype, we can approach transitions as opportunities for growth rather than obstacles to overcome.

Acknowledge the Cycle You're In:

1. Reflect on whether you are currently in a phase of birth (new beginnings), death (endings), or rebirth (transformation). Understanding where you are in the cycle can help you align with the moment's energy and move forward with clarity.

Honor the Process:

1. Each phase of the cycle has its wisdom and lessons. Resist the urge to rush through or bypass challenging emotions, trusting that the Black Madonna holds space for your entire journey.

Seek Support:

1. The Black Madonna's maternal energy reminds us that we cannot navigate life's transitions alone. When needed, we can turn to supportive relationships, spiritual practices, or professional guidance, knowing that reaching out is an act of strength.

Celebrate Growth:

1. When you reach the end of a cycle, celebrate your growth and honor the lessons you've learned. Acknowledging your journey fosters self-compassion and prepares you for the next phase of life.

Real-World Applications

The Black Madonna's archetype has inspired countless individuals to navigate life's transitions with resilience and grace. Pilgrims to her shrines often leave tokens of gratitude for guidance through difficult periods. At the same time, modern spiritual practitioners draw on her symbolism to find meaning in their growth cycles.

The Black Madonna offers a timeless source of wisdom for those undergoing significant life changes—such as career shifts, relationship transitions, or personal transformations. Her stories and rituals provide a framework for embracing change as a sacred process, empowering us to approach life's transitions with courage, authenticity, and faith in renewal cycles.

By aligning with the Black Madonna's energy, we can learn to honor every stage of life's journey, finding strength and purpose in the rhythms of birth, death, and rebirth. Through her example, we are reminded that transformation is not a single moment but a continuous, sacred dance that defines our lives.

THE WISDOM OF LETTING GO

Lessons On Surrendering Through Her Connection To Death And Renewal

With her deep ties to the cycles of death and renewal, the Black Madonna embodies the wisdom of letting go. Her image and stories remind us that surrender is not a loss of power but a profound act of trust in the transformative process of life. She teaches us that to grow, we must release what no longer serves us—relationships, beliefs, patterns, or attachments—and trust that something new will emerge from the space we create.

Letting go can be one of life's most challenging lessons. It often requires facing fears of the unknown and relinquishing the illusion of control. Yet the Black Madonna, with her grounding presence and connection to the sacred shadow, provides a safe container for this process. Her archetype guides us through the pain of release, showing us how to embrace surrender as a holy act of renewal.

The Role Of Death In Transformation

Death plays a central role in the Black Madonna's literal and metaphorical symbolism. Whether depicted in her sorrowful gaze as the *Mater Dolorosa* (Mother of Sorrows) or her earthy, grounded presence, she acknowledges death as not an end but a necessary phase of transformation.

In many spiritual traditions, death represents a purification process—stripping away what is no longer needed to reveal the essence of what remains. The Black Madonna teaches us that letting go is an act of faith, trusting that there is purpose and renewal even in loss. She shows us how to grieve what is gone while holding space for the rebirth that inevitably follows.

Lesson: True surrender involves honoring the pain of loss without resisting or bypassing it. The Black Madonna reminds us that facing and feeling our grief is essential to healing and growth.

Practical Advice: When you struggle to let go, sit silently with an image of the Black Madonna. Acknowledge the loss or change, allowing your emotions to surface. Repeat the affirmation: *"In surrender, I find strength. In a release, I create space for renewal."*

Letting Go of Attachments

The Black Madonna's dark, earthy energy invites us to release attachments to what no longer aligns with our highest good. These attachments may be limiting beliefs, toxic relationships, or outdated versions of ourselves. Letting go does not mean denying the value of what came before but recognizing when it has served its purpose and must be released to make room for something new.

Her connection to nature underscores the inevitability of this process. Trees shed their leaves in the fall, not out of loss but to conserve energy and prepare for growth in the spring. In the same way, the Black Madonna encourages us to trust the wisdom of our inner cycles and embrace the necessity of release.

Lesson: Letting go is not a rejection but an act of self-care and alignment. It creates space for growth and allows us to move forward unburdened.

Practical advice: Create a release ritual when you feel weighed down by attachments. Write down what you need to let go of on slips of paper, then safely burn or bury them as an offering to the Black Madonna. Visualize her energy, helping you release these attachments with love and grace.

Surrendering To The Unknown

One of the most profound lessons the Black Madonna offers is the ability to surrender to the unknown. Her connection to the shadow and the mysteries of life teaches us that we do not need to have all the answers. Instead, we are invited to trust the transformation process, even when the path forward is unclear.

Surrendering to the unknown requires faith—not in external circumstances but in the wisdom of life itself. With her enigmatic and grounding presence, the Black Madonna reminds us that even in the darkest moments, we are held and guided. She encourages us to release the need for certainty and lean into the sacred mystery of what lies ahead.

Lesson: Surrender is an act of trust in life's unfolding. It allows us to move beyond fear and control, opening the door to new possibilities.

Practical advice: When facing uncertainty, light a black candle at your altar and meditate. Imagine placing your fears and doubts into the hands of the Black Madonna, trusting her to carry them for you. End with the affirmation: *"I release what I cannot control and trust in the wisdom of life."*

Practical Steps To Embrace Letting Go

Reflect On What No Longer Serves You:

1. Take time to identify areas where you feel resistance or heaviness. Ask yourself, "What am I holding onto out of fear or habit that no longer aligns with who I am becoming?"

Create a Ritual of Release:

1. Honor the process of letting go with a meaningful ritual. This could involve writing down what you're releasing, performing a symbolic act like burning or burying the paper, or simply speaking your intention aloud.

Allow Space for Grief:

1. Letting go often accompanies grief, even when the release is for our highest good. The Black Madonna reminds us to honor our emotions and give ourselves the time and space to process them.

Trust the Process of Renewal:

1. Focus on the possibilities ahead rather than the void left by what has been released. Create affirmations or intentions that reflect your trust in the life cycle, such as: *"With every ending comes a new beginning."*

Real-World Applications

The wisdom of letting go, as embodied by the Black Madonna, is particularly relevant in times of personal or collective upheaval. Whether navigating career changes, the end of a relationship, or losing an old identity, her teachings provide a framework for facing transitions with courage and grace.

Modern spiritual practices inspired by the Black Madonna often include grief ceremonies, shadow work, and rituals of release, all of which help participants embrace surrender as an act of empowerment. Her presence reminds us that even in the midst of uncertainty, we are held by the cycles of death and renewal, moving toward a greater sense of wholeness.

By aligning with the Black Madonna's energy, we can learn to release what no longer serves us with love, trust the unfolding of life, and step into the next chapter of our journey with openness and strength.

HOW SHE GUIDES US INTO THE LIGHT

Moving From Darkness To Clarity Under Her Guidance

With her deep ties to shadow and mystery, the Black Madonna is a powerful guide for moving from darkness into light. Her archetype reflects the journey through uncertainty, struggle, and transformation, leading to a place of clarity, wisdom, and renewal. Unlike symbols of pure light that often deny the importance of the shadow, the Black Madonna embraces both. She teaches us that light is most potent when it emerges from the depths of darkness, born of courage, introspection, and surrender.

Her duality invites us to honor the cycles of life, where periods of confusion or difficulty are not failures but essential steps in our growth. Under her guidance, we learn to navigate darkness with trust and patience, knowing that the path to clarity and empowerment often requires walking through the shadows.

Embracing Darkness As A Source Of Insight

L literal and metaphorical darkness is often misunderstood as something to be avoided or feared. Yet the Black Madonna's presence reminds us that darkness is a sacred space of potential and transformation. As seeds germinate in the soil and stars shine brightest in the night sky, our most profound insights often arise from moments of uncertainty or pain.

In her connection to the shadow self, the Black Madonna guides us to explore the hidden parts of ourselves that hold wisdom and truth. By confronting our fears, doubts, and unresolved emotions, we move closer to understanding who we are.

Lesson: Darkness is not the absence of light but a space for reflection, healing, and preparation. The Black Madonna encourages us to trust the process of growth that occurs in life's unseen spaces.

Practical advice: When facing moments of confusion or struggle, journal or meditate on the question, *"What is this darkness trying to teach me?"* Imagine the Black Madonna sitting with you, offering her steady presence as you reflect.

Trusting The Process Of Transformation

Transformation is rarely straightforward or easy. The journey from darkness to light often involves letting go of the familiar, facing uncertainty, and embracing vulnerability. As a figure of death and rebirth, the Black Madonna teaches us to trust this process, even when the path forward is unclear.

Her maternal energy provides reassurance that we are never alone in this journey. She reminds us that the light we seek is not something external but something we carry within. Through her guidance, we learn to nurture our inner light, even when it feels faint, and trust that it will grow stronger with time.

Lesson: Transformation requires patience and trust. The Black Madonna teaches us to embrace the journey, knowing that every step—no matter how small—leads us closer to clarity and renewal.

Practical Advice: Practice patience during periods of transition. Use a mantra like *"I trust the process of my transformation"* to stay grounded and focused. Light a candle as a symbol of your inner light, allowing its flame to remind you of your resilience.

Emerging Into The Light

The Black Madonna's stories often include themes of miraculous discovery or emergence. Whether found in a cave, a river, or a hidden corner of the earth, her statues symbolize the light of the divine feminine arising from darkness. These narratives mirror our potential to emerge from life's challenges with greater clarity, strength, and wisdom.

Emerging into the light does not mean erasing the past but integrating its lessons. The Black Madonna's ability to hold both shadow and illumination teaches us that clarity comes not from denying our struggles but from embracing them as part of our journey.

Lesson: The light we seek is often found within the lessons of the shadows. The Black Madonna shows us that we emerge more substantial and whole by facing and integrating our experiences.

Practical Advice: Celebrate moments of clarity and growth as milestones on your journey. Spend time reflecting on what you've learned from periods of darkness, and express gratitude for the insights they've brought. Create a ritual of emergence by lighting a white candle and affirming your readiness to step into the next phase of your life.

Practical Steps For Moving From Darkness To Clarity

Acknowledge The Darkness:

1. Honor the emotions, challenges, or uncertainties you are experiencing without judgment. The Black Madonna's archetype reminds us that acknowledging the darkness is the first step toward transformation.

Seek Inner Guidance:

1. The Black Madonna represents the wisdom of the divine feminine, which is deeply intuitive. Use meditation, prayer, or journaling to access your inner guidance, trusting that clarity will come in time.

Create a Symbolic Light:

1. Use physical symbols, such as candles or crystals, to represent the light you are moving toward. Let these symbols remind you of your inner strength and resilience.

Celebrate Small Steps:

1. Transformation doesn't happen all at once. Celebrate the small moments of insight, progress, or healing that mark your journey from darkness to light.

Lean on Her Presence:

1. Imagine the Black Madonna walking beside you during difficult times, her steady presence offering support. Use affirmations like *"I am held in her embrace as I find my way to clarity."*

Real-World Applications

The Black Madonna's guidance in moving from darkness to light resonates deeply in modern life, where uncertainty and change are constant. Her archetype is often invoked during times of personal crisis, such as grief, career transitions, or identity shifts, offering reassurance that clarity and renewal are possible.

In spiritual retreats and women's circles, her stories and rituals help participants navigate periods of transformation, encouraging them to trust the process and embrace the wisdom that emerges from shadow work.

By working with the Black Madonna's energy, we learn to see darkness not as a barrier but as an invitation to explore, heal, and grow. Her archetype inspires us to trust that light will always emerge, guiding us toward clarity, purpose, and a deeper connection to ourselves and the divine.

10: THE BLACK MADONNA'S RELEVANCE TODAY

"In the sacred spaces where her image rests, time bends, and the mysteries of the goddess unfold, connecting us to the heart of the universe."

A LIVING ARCHETYPE IN THE MODERN WORLD

WHY HER SYMBOLISM ENDURES

How Her Mysteries Are Still Relevant In Today's Spiritual And Cultural Landscapes

The Black Madonna's symbolism has transcended centuries, remaining profoundly relevant in the modern world. She is not a relic of the past but a living archetype whose mysteries continue to speak to the heart of contemporary spiritual and cultural concerns. In an age marked by rapid change, social upheaval, and a growing yearning for deeper connection, the Black Madonna is a potent reminder of resilience, transformation, and the sacred balance between shadow and light.

Her enduring appeal lies in her ability to embody paradoxes:

she is motherly yet fierce, sorrowful yet hopeful, ancient yet timeless. Her mysteries invite us to explore the depths of our inner world while remaining engaged with the struggles and beauty of life. Whether through her connection to the divine feminine, her symbolism of inclusivity, or her role as a guide through life's transitions, the Black Madonna remains a beacon of wisdom, healing, and empowerment for spiritual seekers worldwide.

The Black Madonna As A Symbol Of The Divine Feminine

There is a collective call to reclaim the divine feminine in today's world. This movement seeks to rebalance spiritual and societal values by honoring intuition, nurturing, creativity, and inclusivity. With her maternal yet mysterious presence, the Black Madonna embodies this feminine power in its fullest expression.

Her dark skin and connection to the earth challenge conventional images of the divine, reminding us that divinity is not confined to perfection or light but also dwells in the shadows and complexities of life. She invites us to embrace the fullness of our humanity, including the parts that have been suppressed or marginalized.

In modern spiritual practices, the Black Madonna inspires a return to intuitive wisdom, cyclical living, and deep reverence for the natural world. She encourages seekers to honor their inner feminine energy, whether through creative expression, nurturing relationships, or practices that restore balance and connection. These practices could include meditation, nature walks, or creative writing.

Relevance Today: The Black Madonna's archetype aligns with movements advocating for feminine empowerment, environmental sustainability, and healing patriarchal wounds. Her presence speaks to the need for a more holistic and compassionate way of living that integrates feminine and masculine energies.

Inclusivity And The Black Madonna

The Black Madonna's image—marked by her dark skin—has long resonated with marginalized communities. For many, she represents a divine figure who understands the struggles of the oppressed, the forgotten, and the overlooked. In today's conversations about diversity, equity, and inclusion, her symbolism offers a powerful reminder of the sacredness of all people, regardless of race, culture, or background.

Historically, communities seeking solace and justice have embraced the Black Madonna. In Latin America, Afro-Brazilian and indigenous groups have venerated her as a protector and healer, often blending her image with ancestral deities. In Europe, she has been a symbol of resilience during war and hardship, offering hope to those who feel unseen.

In a modern context, the Black Madonna's inclusivity challenges us to expand our spiritual frameworks to embrace all aspects of humanity. She teaches us that divinity exists in diversity and that honoring different perspectives and experiences enriches our collective understanding.

Relevance Today: The Black Madonna's inclusive energy aligns with contemporary efforts to decolonize spirituality and embrace intersectionality. Her image reminds us that true empowerment comes from uplifting all voices and celebrating the beauty of difference.

Navigating Life's Uncertainty

The Black Madonna's deep connection to the shadow and transformation makes her especially relevant in a world of uncertainty. Her symbolism of death, renewal, and the integration of light and darkness resonates with those seeking meaning and purpose amid chaos.

In the face of global crises—climate change, political instability, and widespread mental health challenges—the Black Madonna reminds us of the resilience of the human spirit. Her presence encourages us to confront fear, grief, and doubt, trusting that even the darkest times hold the potential for growth and renewal.

Modern spiritual seekers turn to her as a guide through personal and collective transitions, finding solace in her ability to hold space for pain and hope. Her archetype teaches us to surrender to the unknown, embrace life's cycles, and emerge more substantial and grounded. These 'collective transitions' could include societal changes, such as the transition to a more sustainable world, or personal changes, such as the transition to a new phase of life.

Relevance Today: The Black Madonna's wisdom is a balm for an anxious world, offering tools for navigating uncertainty with courage and grace. Her connection to transformation and rebirth resonates with those seeking to rebuild their lives or communities after loss or change.

Practical Applications Of Her Symbolism

The Black Madonna's enduring relevance is not just theoretical; it manifests in tangible ways in the modern world. Her image and teachings inspire a wide range of spiritual and cultural practices that address today's challenges:

1. **Personal Empowerment:** Her archetype inspires individuals to embrace their inner strength, integrate their shadows, and navigate life's transitions with resilience.

2. **Feminine Leadership:** The Black Madonna's nurturing yet fierce energy offers a leadership model that values compassion, collaboration, and intuition.

3. **Social Justice Movements:** Her role as a protector of the oppressed aligns with contemporary efforts to create a more just and equitable society. Activists often draw on her image as a source of inspiration and strength.

Healing Practices: Therapists, healers, and spiritual teachers incorporate the Black Madonna into shadow work, grief rituals, and other transformative practices, offering a beacon of hope and comfort to those confronting deep wounds.

Art and Creativity: Her mysteries inspire artists, musicians, and writers who use her image and symbolism to explore themes of empowerment, diversity, and the sacred feminine, sparking creativity and inspiration.

Why Her Symbolism Endures

The Black Madonna's endurance lies in her ability to meet us where we are. She is not confined by dogma or tradition but evolves with the needs of each generation. Her archetype speaks to universal experiences—birth, death, renewal, struggle, and triumph—making her relevant across cultures, spiritual paths, and personal journeys.

The Black Madonna offers a sacred mirror for our times in a world seeking more profound connection, healing, and meaning. Her mysteries remind us that transformation is possible, that shadow and light coexist, and that divinity is present in every aspect of our lives.

Her enduring wisdom calls for modern seekers to be ready to embrace their wholeness, heal their wounds, and step into a more authentic and empowered way of being.

THE BLACK MADONNA AND SOCIAL JUSTICE

Her Influence As A Figure Of Resilience And Activism

The Black Madonna has long been associated with resilience, protection, and the empowerment of the oppressed, making her a potent symbol of social justice. Across cultures, she is revered as a mother to the marginalized, a protector of the downtrodden, and a guiding force for those seeking equity and liberation. Her enduring presence reminds us that spirituality and activism are not separate paths but deeply intertwined.

The Black Madonna is a beacon of hope and resilience in the modern world, where systemic inequalities, environmental crises, and social movements dominate the global narrative. Her energy calls on us to confront injustice with courage, nurture healing within our communities, and use our unique voices to create a more just and compassionate world.

Historical Ties To Justice And Liberation

The Black Madonna's influence on social justice is rooted in her historical role as a protector of the oppressed. Throughout history, her image has been invoked during social and political upheaval periods, offering solace and strength to those fighting for their rights.

- **Haiti:** In Vodou traditions, the Black Madonna is syncretized with *Erzulie Dantor*, a fierce protector of women and children. During the Haitian Revolution (1791–1804), *Erzulie Dantor* was a spiritual rallying figure for enslaved people seeking freedom. Her association with justice and liberation persists in modern Haitian culture, where she is honored for her strength and advocacy for the oppressed.

- **Poland:** The Black Madonna of Częstochowa symbolized Polish resistance during the 17th century when she was credited with protecting the Jasna Góra Monastery from invaders. Later, she was embraced as a national symbol during the Solidarity movement in the 1980s, a peaceful uprising against communist rule.

- **Latin America:** In Brazil, *Nossa Senhora Aparecida* (Our Lady of Aparecida) patronizes the poor and marginalized. Her miracles, often tied to the struggles of everyday people, have made her a beloved symbol of hope and justice.

In these examples, the Black Madonna embodies resilience, inspiring people to stand firm in the face of oppression while nurturing a vision of liberation and equality.

The Black Madonna As A Guide For Modern Activism

In the context of modern social justice movements, the Black Madonna's archetype offers both inspiration and guidance. Her connection to the shadow reminds us to confront the uncomfortable truths of inequality, while her nurturing energy encourages us to approach activism with compassion and care.

Resilience In The Face Of Injustice:

1. The Black Madonna's presence calls on activists to remain steadfast, even when progress feels slow, or resistance seems overwhelming. Her stories of miraculous interventions remind us that persistence and faith can lead to transformation.

Practical advice: Before engaging in advocacy, draw on her energy by creating a small ritual. Light a black candle and pray for her guidance, asking for the strength to persevere and the wisdom to act with integrity.

Compassionate Leadership:

1. The Black Madonna's maternal qualities inspire a model of leadership rooted in compassion, care, and inclusivity. She reminds us that social change is not about domination but about uplifting and healing

communities.

Practical Advice: As you lead or participate in social justice efforts, prioritize collaboration and empathy. Reflect on how your actions can create spaces for healing and empowerment rather than division.

Healing Collective Wounds:

1. Social justice is about dismantling systems of oppression and healing the collective wounds they have caused. The Black Madonna's connection to grief and renewal makes her a powerful ally in this work. She encourages us to acknowledge the pain of the past while envisioning a better future.

Practical Advice: Host a collective healing circle inspired by the Black Madonna. Include moments of reflection, storytelling, and shared rituals to honor the pain and resilience of those affected by injustice.

A Symbol Of Intersectionality

The Black Madonna's dark complexion and connection to marginalized communities make her a symbol of intersectionality, a framework that recognizes how various forms of oppression—such as race, gender, and class—intersect to create unique experiences of discrimination. Her image calls on us to address these overlapping injustices, ensuring no one is excluded from pursuing equality.

In modern feminist movements, the Black Madonna serves as an inclusive and multifaceted archetype of feminine empowerment. She represents women of all backgrounds and experiences and challenges narrow definitions of femininity and divinity.

Relevance Today: Activists working within intersectional frameworks can draw on the Black Madonna's energy to create movements that uplift all voices, particularly those historically excluded or silenced. Her image reminds us that justice is incomplete without inclusivity.

Practical Ways To Connect Her Energy With Social Justice

Invoke Her in Advocacy Work:

1. Before participating in protests, community organizing, or acts of advocacy, call on the Black Madonna for guidance. Light a candle and pray for protection, resilience, and clarity in your efforts.

Create Art for Change:

1. Use her image or symbolism to inspire art, writing, or performances that address social justice themes. Creative expression can be a powerful tool for raising awareness and fostering connection.

Host Rituals for Collective Action:

1. Gather like-minded individuals to honor the Black Madonna through shared rituals, such as lighting candles for victims of injustice or meditating on solutions to systemic issues.

Support Marginalized Communities:

1. Channel the Black Madonna's energy by actively

2. supporting organizations and initiatives that advocate for marginalized groups. Volunteer, donate, or use your platform to amplify their voices.

Real-World Examples

The Black Madonna continues to inspire activists, artists, and leaders worldwide. From feminist movements reclaiming the divine feminine to grassroots organizations advocating for justice, her archetype serves as a unifying force for those seeking to create a more equitable society.

In places like Haiti, Brazil, and Poland, her shrines remain sites of pilgrimage and prayer for those grappling with social and political challenges. Modern spiritual communities often invoke her as a patroness of justice, holding rituals and ceremonies in her honor to foster resilience and hope.

Her influence is also seen in contemporary art and literature, where she is celebrated as a symbol of empowerment and transformation. Artists and writers often use her image to explore themes of resistance, healing, and liberation, ensuring that her legacy inspires future generations.

Why Her Influence Endures In Social Justice

The Black Madonna's relevance to social justice lies in her ability to bridge the spiritual and the practical. She offers a source of strength and inspiration and a framework for approaching activism with compassion, resilience, and inclusivity.

In a world hungry for healing and transformation, her

archetype reminds us that change begins with courage and care. She calls on us to stand with the oppressed, nurture our communities, and trust in the power of collective action. Through her guidance, we learn that justice is not just a goal but a sacred path—one that honors the dignity, strength, and divinity of all people.

THE CALL TO EMBODY THE BLACK MADONNA

How Individuals Can Bring Her Energy Into Their Own Lives And Communities

The Black Madonna is more than a symbol to revere—she is an archetype to embody. Her energy calls on us to integrate her qualities of strength, compassion, resilience, and inclusivity into our own lives and communities. By walking in her footsteps, we honor her legacy and contribute to the healing, transformation, and empowerment she represents.

To embody the Black Madonna means to embrace the paradoxes she holds: being both nurturing and fierce, shadowed and illuminated, deeply rooted and transcendent. It requires courage to face our shadows, compassion to serve others, and the willingness to stand as protectors of justice and caretakers of the sacred. In bringing her energy into our lives, we become agents of the change, healing, and balance she inspires.

1. Embrace Shadow Work And Inner Transformation

The Black Madonna's connection to the shadow reminds us that personal growth begins with self-awareness. Embodying her energy means confronting our inner darkness—fears, insecurities, and unhealed wounds—and transforming these aspects into sources of strength and wisdom.

Practical advice:

- Dedicate time for self-reflection and shadow work. Use journaling or meditation to explore the parts of yourself you tend to suppress or avoid.

- Practice self-compassion as you confront your shadow, remembering that the Black Madonna holds space for all aspects of your being.

- Create a transformation ritual, such as lighting a candle to symbolize bringing light to your shadows.

2. Nurture Resilience In Times Of Change

Life's challenges often call for resilience, and the Black Madonna teaches us to draw strength from within, even in moments of uncertainty. Embodying her energy means embracing life's cycles of death and rebirth, trusting in the renewal process, and remaining grounded through transitions.

Practical Advice:

- Cultivate resilience by grounding yourself in daily spiritual practices, such as prayer, meditation, or gratitude journaling.

- Turn to her image or energy during times of difficulty. Visualize her as a steady presence guiding you through the unknown.

- Affirm your strength with mantras such as, *"I am resilient. I grow stronger with every challenge I face."*

3. Serve As A Protector And Advocate

The Black Madonna is a fierce protector of the vulnerable, a role we are called to embody in our communities. Whether through advocacy, mentorship, or small acts of kindness, living her energy means standing up for those in need and fostering a sense of safety and belonging.

Practical Advice:

- Identify ways to support your community, such as volunteering at a shelter, mentoring youth, or advocating for social justice causes.

- Be a voice for those who cannot speak for themselves, using your platform to amplify marginalized voices.

- Protect your relationships by creating safe spaces for others to express themselves without judgment.

4. Cultivate Creativity And Intuition

The Black Madonna's energy is profoundly creative and intuitive, tied to the mysteries of the divine feminine. Embodying her means honoring your creative potential and trusting your inner wisdom, even when it challenges conventional thinking.

Practical Advice:

- Engage in creative practices that inspire you through art, writing, dance, or music. Dedicate these acts to the Black Madonna as a form of devotion.

- Listen to your inner voice and honor your instincts to strengthen your intuition. Spend time in silence or nature to deepen this connection.

- Create a vision board or sacred space to celebrate your creative goals and dreams, allowing the Black Madonna's energy to guide you.

5. Build Inclusive And Healing Communities

The Black Madonna's inclusivity and role as a unifier inspire us to create spaces where everyone feels seen, valued, and supported. Embodying her energy means fostering communities that uplift diverse voices and prioritize healing and connection.

Practical Advice:

- Host gatherings or circles where people can share their stories and experiences in a supportive environment. Use rituals inspired by the Black Madonna to foster connection and healing.

- Educate yourself about the experiences of marginalized groups and work to create more inclusive spaces in your personal and professional life.

- Advocate for equitable practices in your community, workplace, or spiritual circles, ensuring all voices are heard and honored.

6. Honor The Sacred In Everyday Life

The Black Madonna's presence reminds us to find the sacred in the ordinary. By embodying her energy, we infuse our daily lives with mindfulness, gratitude, and reverence for the beauty of existence.

Practical Advice:

- Begin each day with gratitude, dedicating your day to the Black Madonna and the qualities she represents.

- Create small rituals to honor the sacred, such as lighting candles during meals, praying before starting work, or spending time in nature.

- Approach your daily tasks with intention and mindfulness, seeing each moment as an opportunity to embody her energy.

Real-World Applications

The call to embody the Black Madonna is being answered in diverse ways worldwide. Spiritual practitioners integrate her energy into personal development workshops, creative retreats, and activism. Feminist movements draw on her archetype to inspire empowerment and equity, while community leaders use her stories to foster resilience and hope in challenging times.

Individuals honor her personally by embracing their complexity, nurturing their creativity, and building bridges of connection within their families and communities. Through her guidance, people find the strength to face challenges, the compassion to support others, and the courage to pursue their dreams.

Why Embodying The Black Madonna Matters

Embodying the Black Madonna means actively participating in her legacy of healing, transformation, and empowerment. It is a call to integrate her wisdom into our actions, thoughts, and relationships, bringing her energy into a modern world that deeply needs it.

By walking with her qualities—resilience, inclusivity, creativity, and compassion—we transform ourselves and inspire change in those around us. Through her, we learn that living a life of purpose, authenticity, and connection is our most sacred offering.

CONCLUSION

Printed in Dunstable, United Kingdom